Table of Contents

D0509487

Comprehensive Reading and Writing Assessment Grade 8

Product Development: Atlantic Group, Barrington, RI

Editor: Jennifer DePino

Design: Reynolds Design and Management, Waltham, MA

Typesetting/Art: LMY Studio, Inc., Winchester, MA

Contributing Writers: Jean Sullivan-Beall, Josh Brackett, Lois Mortimer, Myka-Lynne Sokoloff

Consultants: Sheldon Shuch, Ph.D.

George H. Campbell, Jr., M.Ed.

Photo Credits: © Hulton-Deutsch Collection/Corbis: pages 13, and 91. © The Museum of the City of New York/Corbis: pages 12, 14, 90 and 94. © The Royal Geographical Society, London: pages 35, 36, 37, 39, 122, 123, and 124. Raymond Gehman/Corbis: pages 40, 42, and 133. © Corbis: pages 41, 134, and 143.

ISBN: 1-56936-903-8

© 2002 OPTIONS Publishing, Inc.

P.O. Box 1749

Merrimack, NH 02054-1749

TOLL FREE: 800-782-7300 ■ FAX: 603-424-4056

www.optionspublishing.com

All rights reserved. Printed in the USA. No part of this document may be reproduced or used by any means— graphic, electronic, or mechanical—including photocopying, recording, taping, and information storage and retrieval systems—without written permission of the publisher.

15 14 13 12 11 10 9 8 7 6 5 4 3 2

©2002 Options Publishing, Inc.

DAYTON MEMORIAL LIBRARY
REGIS UNIVERSITY
3333 REGIS BLVD.,
DENVER, CO 80221

No copying permitted.

To the Student

In this book, you will find two practice tests: Test A and Test B. After you take each test, you will check your answers by using the **Instruction for Test A** beginning on page 67 and **Instruction for Test B** beginning on page 121. These pages help you understand why your answers are correct or incorrect. These pages also give you **Strategies and Tips** to help you understand each skill that is tested. The **TRY IT!** activities also provide additional practice.

Strategies and Tips for Taking the Test

- *Listen carefully* as your teacher reads the directions aloud. Be sure to read *all* the directions at the beginning of each test. It is important to ask your teacher to explain any directions that you do not understand.

- Carefully *read* each selection. Carefully *listen* when your teacher reads a selection aloud. When you answer the questions, you may look back at the reading selections or your notes for the listening selection as often as you like.

- Each test session has a time limit. *Plan your time.* To budget your time for each part of the test, look quickly through the entire session before you begin answering questions.

- The Reading and Listening and Writing Sessions have open-ended questions. Be sure to *support or explain your answer* to these questions by including details from the reading or listening selection.

 This symbol means that your writing will also be scored for how well you use grammar, punctuation, paragraphs, and spelling. Whenever you see this symbol, be sure to check your writing.

Tests A and B ask you to write about what you have listened to or read. Your writing will **not** be scored on your personal opinions. It **will** be scored on

- how clearly you organize your answers
- how carefully and completely you answer each question
- how correctly you use grammar, paragraphs, punctuation, and spelling

- how well you support your ideas with facts and examples
- how interesting and pleasant your written answers are to read

Directions for Reading Session

In this part of the test, you are going to read a story, an article, and a journal. As you answer the questions about what you have read, you may look back at the selections as often as you like.

Now begin reading.

Student Name _____

©2002 Options Publishing, Inc.

No copying permitted.

Here is a story about a message in a fortune cookie and how that message influences a young girl. Read "The Fortune Cookie." Then answer Numbers 1 through 8.

THE FORTUNE COOKIE

"Let me read mine now, Mom!" cried Quan, pushing away his empty plate. "'A stitch in time saves nine.'"

"That's easy," laughed Mrs. Li. "If you do your homework as soon as it's assigned, it will save you a lot of worry in the future. Min, what words of advice does yours give?"

Min looked around the circle of happy faces at the table. It was a family tradition to celebrate birthdays at the local Chinese Restaurant, and today she was thirteen years old. The climax of the meal was the sharing of their fortune cookies, and the linen cloth was littered with crumbs and the discarded words of wisdom. "No, I want to keep mine until I have figured out what it means for myself," Min said. She placed the slip of paper carefully in her purse. Min had the feeling that it meant something special.

The following day was Saturday. "No school," Min said happily to herself, as she curled her toes under the blanket. The sun was shining through the windows and she, Carol, and her friends had planned a picnic down in the park. The whole day seemed to stretch invitingly before her.

"Min, are you awake?" Her mother's voice roused her from her daydreams. "Get up, hon, I want you to go on an errand for me."

"Oh Mom, what is it?" Reluctantly Min dragged herself into the kitchen.

"Do me a favor and take these groceries across to Mrs. Spencer. She has hurt her back and is having difficulty going to the stores right now." Min pulled on jeans and a T-shirt, ran a comb through her short dark hair, picked up the groceries, and dashed across the street. She knocked impatiently on her neighbor's back door and went in—not waiting to be invited. However, as she placed the brown paper bag on the kitchen table, something prompted her to put her head around the

©2002 Options Publishing, Inc.

living room door. The drapes were still closed, and the room was in darkness. Min padded across to the hallway and called gently, "Mrs. Spencer, it's Min. Mom sent over some groceries."

A faint voice answered from a bedroom upstairs. "Thank you, Min. Please excuse me if I don't come down to greet you."

"Mrs. Spencer, are you all right? May I come up?"

From the bedroom doorway, Min smiled shyly at her silver-haired neighbor. She looked frailer and more fragile than Min remembered her. "Mrs. Spencer, you don't look well. Can I fix you some breakfast?" She could see from the look of relief on Mrs. Spencer's face that this was a very welcome offer. "Oh well," Min thought, "Carol would wait for half an hour."

Min carried the tray of eggs, toast, and coffee upstairs, intending to leave it and scoot home, but on an impulse, or whim, she found herself asking, "Mrs. Spencer, would you like me to collect your mail?" Minutes later she had plumped up the pillows and made Mrs. Spencer comfortable with the tray. As Min put the letters and newspaper next to Mrs. Spencer, it struck her that something was not quite right. "Mrs. Spencer, where are your reading glasses?"

"I'm afraid I broke them, dear, when I fell. I do feel so helpless without them."

Hours later, when Mrs. Li came across to see what had happened to her daughter, she found Min and Mrs. Spencer curled up together on the bed, deep in conversation. Opened letters and discarded newspapers lay beside them.

"It was really sweet of you to give up your day to help Mrs. Spencer," Min's mother said as they made their way across the street. "Carol called to say that they couldn't wait for you any longer."

"It's all right, Mom. I guess I understand my fortune cookie now." Min smiled as she took it out of her purse and put it on the dressing table. She recited it quietly to herself: "The more you give away, the more you have."

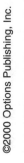

Go on

1 What is the author's general purpose in writing this article?

Ⓐ to entertain readers with an amusing story

Ⓑ to explain how an experience can change a person's outlook on life

Ⓒ to describe how plans for a day can quickly change

Ⓓ to persuade readers to take groceries to their neighbors

2 "The Fortune Cookie" can best be described as a work

Ⓕ of nonfiction that gives the reader facts about a subject.

Ⓖ of fiction, but the characters seem real, and the events could have happened.

Ⓗ of nonfiction that tries to persuade a reader to think a certain way.

Ⓙ of nonfiction that gives facts and information about a real person.

3 You can draw the conclusion that Min

Ⓐ is unhappy that she spent her birthday at the restaurant.

Ⓑ will spend every Saturday with Mrs. Spencer.

Ⓒ annoyed Mrs. Spencer by staying with her all day.

Ⓓ was not disappointed that she had missed the picnic.

4 You can infer that Min stayed with Mrs. Spencer because

Ⓕ Min could tell that Mrs. Spencer really needed help and companionship.

Ⓖ Min's mother wanted her to stay.

Ⓗ Min did not want to spend the entire day with friends.

Ⓙ Min felt guilty about leaving Mrs. Spencer because she was ill.

©2002 Options Publishing, Inc.

5 Mrs. Spencer cannot go to the store because

(A) she hurt her back.

(B) she does not drive.

(C) her reading glasses are broken.

(D) she is expecting a visit from Min.

6 Which of the following statements is a *valid* generalization?

(F) Everyone in Mrs. Spencer's neighborhood liked her.

(G) All people love to celebrate birthdays.

(H) Fortune cookies often contain thought-provoking sayings.

(J) Everyone can help the elderly at the senior center.

7 Which of the following statements is an opinion?

(A) Carol called to say that they couldn't wait any longer for Min.

(B) Mrs. Spencer hurt her back.

(C) Min was pleased with herself for helping Mrs. Spencer.

(D) Min and her friends had planned a picnic in the park.

8 "Mrs. Spencer looked *frailer* and more fragile than Min remembered her." The word *frailer* means

(F) stronger.

(G) healthier.

(H) weaker.

(J) tougher.

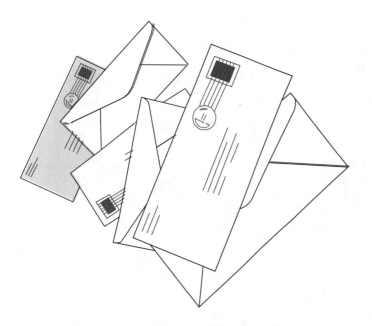

Go on

No copying permitted.

©2002 Options Publishing, Inc.

Directions

Here is an article about software that allows you to talk to a computer.
Read "A Computer to Talk To." Then answer Numbers 9 through 18.

A COMPUTER TO TALK TO

Richard knew the Karachi airport and the airspace around it well, having taken off from here several times before. His checklist complete, he adjusted his headset, glanced at the cockpit dials, and looked down the runway.

"Tower, Cessna 916, Runway 14," he said. "Request takeoff clearance."

"Cleared for takeoff," came the reply in his earpiece. The voice was female. The accent was Pakistani. Richard opened the throttle.

Then his mother came into the room. "I know you love that computer game, but it's time to stop playing and start your homework."

The game Richard was playing is a flight simulator game that allows the player to experience what it is like to fly. It has two software improvements: One improvement stores and plays 25,000 prerecorded audio clips—the stock phrases that air traffic controllers use to communicate with pilots. These clips, or phrases, are spoken in the accented English of controllers in forty different parts of the world. The second improvement is *voice recognition software*. This software translates human speech—the words Richard used—into signals that a computer can understand. The result is that the game gives Richard a true-to-life flight experience. He gets the feeling he is really controlling the plane because the pilot and air traffic controller have conversations that are a natural part of flying.

One goal of the engineers who develop computer systems is to have computers adapt to people rather than have people adapt to computers. This means getting computers to communicate, or talk, in ways that are natural. Computer developers want people to be able to talk to their computers instead of using devices. The keyboard and mouse could be replaced by a person's voice!

Speech is natural for human beings. We learn to speak at an early age. Most computers can play music and produce sound effects. Many can also

©2002 Options Publishing, Inc.

speak words and talk to us. However, getting computers to understand what *we* say to them is very difficult. Why?

Well, to understand speech, a computer must recognize *all* the individual sounds that make up each word. For example, the spoken word *cat* has three sounds. It has a *k* sound at the beginning, a short *a* sound in the middle, and a *t* sound at the end. Think of words that begin with the letter *c* and the different sounds within each word: *cat, cool, chin,* or *ceiling.* And to make matters more difficult, people in different parts of the country or the world speak English with different accents. English also sounds different when spoken in a continuous speech pattern rather than pronouncing each word—One—Word—At—A—Time.

For a computer to sort out all these sounds requires a huge amount of processing power. Only recently has this power been available at affordable prices. So it's no surprise that one of the first games to use voice recognition software can understand only a few sets of phrases—in this case, the phrases that pilots use when they talk to control towers. If you tried to read a poem or a grocery list to the flight simulator game, it wouldn't know what to do!

Systems that understand enough words so that you can talk to them are still very expensive. They require a much more powerful computer than most of us have on our desks. When those systems do become available at affordable prices, some people may still prefer to use the traditional keyboard and mouse. However, many people may like the freedom of using their voice rather than their fingertips on a keyboard. Imagine, you might "speak" your next book report into your computer, and the computer will put your words onto the page! Voice recognition systems will give independence to physically challenged people who cannot type or see the screen or keyboard.

And, for those of us who love computer games, there are some really cool voice-operated games coming!

©2002 Options Publishing, Inc.

No copying permitted.

9 This article is mostly about

Ⓐ computer games.

Ⓑ voice recognition software and what it does.

Ⓒ voice recognition will be useful for physically challenged people.

Ⓓ how people speak English with different accents.

11 Getting computers to understand what we say is difficult because

Ⓐ computers can only speak words.

Ⓑ computer equipment is very expensive.

Ⓒ people do not want computers with voice recognition software.

Ⓓ computers must recognize the separate sounds within every word.

10 Which detail from the article *best* supports the main idea of the article?

Ⓕ Voice recognition software translates human speech into signals that a computer can understand.

Ⓖ The word *cat* is made up of three different sounds.

Ⓗ Most computers can play music and produce sound effects.

Ⓙ The air traffic controller spoke with a Pakistani accent.

12 From the facts in the article, you can conclude that voice recognition software

Ⓕ will always need computers that are too expensive.

Ⓖ will become more popular as powerful computers become less expensive.

Ⓗ will be used only in computer games.

Ⓙ will never be popular because it is too difficult to use.

Go on

©2002 Options Publishing, Inc.

No copying permitted.

13 From the details in the article, you can infer that Richard is taking off from an airport in

Ⓐ England.

Ⓑ the United States.

Ⓒ Pakistan.

Ⓓ Russia.

14 What was one of the software improvements to Richard's flight simulator game?

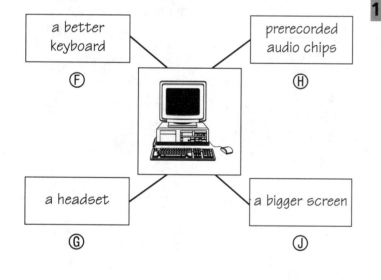

a better keyboard

Ⓕ

prerecorded audio chips

Ⓗ

a headset

Ⓖ

a bigger screen

Ⓙ

15 Which of the following details occurs *first* in the article?

Ⓐ an explanation of what voice recognition software does

Ⓑ an explanation of how words are made up of individual sounds

Ⓒ some people may prefer to use the traditional keyboard and mouse

Ⓓ the flight simulator game can understand only a few sets of phrases

16 Which of the following statements is an opinion?

Ⓕ Speech is natural for human beings. We learn to speak at an early age.

Ⓖ Every word is made up of individual sounds.

Ⓗ Games that use voice recognition software are more fun to play.

Ⓙ Computers that understand spoken words require a huge amount of processing power.

©2002 Options Publishing, Inc.

17 "A Computer to Talk To" can best be described as

Ⓐ a fictional short story.

Ⓑ a biography.

Ⓒ a play.

Ⓓ an article.

18 "Computer developers want people to be able to talk to their computers instead of using *devices*. The keyboard and mouse could be replaced by a person's voice!" The word *devices* means

Ⓕ equipment.

Ⓖ jobs.

Ⓗ computers.

Ⓙ plans.

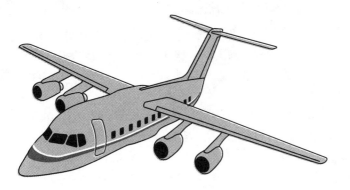

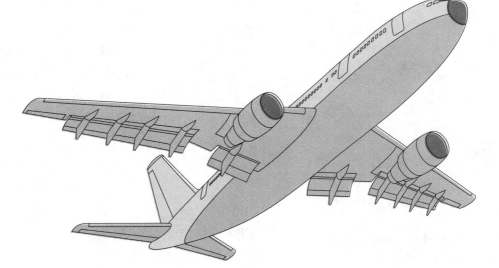

©2002 Options Publishing, Inc.

Go on

Directions

Here is a journal about a woman who learns to navigate a clipper ship during the 1800s. Read "The Journal of Emma Scars." Then answer Numbers 19 through 25.

The Journal of Emma Scars

In the 1800s, sailing ships transported most raw materials and manufactured goods around the world. Whaling boats and tall-masted clipper ships crisscrossed the oceans, sometimes on journeys lasting as long as two years. Often, the wives of the ships' captains traveled with their husbands. Many of these women kept journals or sent letters home describing their adventures at sea.

This journal is called historical fiction. The author took real events from the past and built a fictional character and journal around the events.

◆

May 10, 1849, South Pacific

I write from our cabin somewhere in the South Seas. I am so proud of Edward as he issues orders to trim the sails and bring the ship about. Our ship is quite glorious under sail.

I spend my days writing letters, reading novels, doing Edward's laundry, and supervising the cook. The weather has been lovely and we are making good progress. Most of the seamen are caring and hardworking, although rather rough sorts. They call our ship a "hen frigate," meaning that there is a woman on board. They are not pleased to have me aboard, as they think this will bring bad luck. However, I am determined to change their minds by befriending them, while keeping out of their way.

Why do you suppose that young women are not permitted to attend maritime academies to learn to navigate and command grand ships, such as Edward's? Such skills seem far more stimulating than darning socks and stitching samplers!

The clipper ship *Flying Cloud* sailed in 1851. It is typical of the type of ship Emma and her husband sailed.

©2002 Options Publishing, Inc.

No copying permitted.

June 19, 1849, South Pacific

We have spent three days sitting in the Doldrums, which is a hot, airless calm. Since we have no wind or even a breeze, we cannot make any progress. Edward wears a fierce scowl, worrying constantly about the time we must make up to deliver our cargo.

The crew is bored and restless. To relieve the tedium, the men caught a shark and brought it on board, which entertained us for a few hours and raised the spirits of those on the ship. I still beg Edward to teach me navigation skills, and he has agreed, somewhat reluctantly. He does not think a woman needs to know these things, but he will teach me anyway. We take "sightings" of the stars on clear nights. To navigate, or set a course, for the ship, I must learn a great deal of mathematics and trigonometry, which I truly enjoy.

Typical clothing worn by a Victorian woman.

August 23, 1849, South Pacific

Two nights ago, I stayed up many hours nursing Edward, who is ill with a fever. I was bathing his forehead with a towel soaked in seawater when the first mate came in to announce the sighting of storm clouds. Without Edward to navigate, the men worry about becoming caught in the storm and losing our direction.

I entered the captain's bridge and began my calculations to help us navigate clear of the storm. I gave orders to adjust the sails to catch the breeze and then set our course. I was determined that we should make haste to leave this deadly calm and outrun the storm that chased us. To my amazement, none of the men refused or balked at my command! It was my good fortune to earn their trust and friendship early in the voyage.

Unfortunately, we could not outrun the storm. The main mast snapped with a fierce crack as thunder rolled and lightning struck all around us that night. The men pulled together under my command to shorten the canvas sails and steer us from the crest of one huge wave to the next. I tied myself onto the bridge so that the waves could not sweep me overboard. I have never been so frightened in my life, yet I did not let the men see, for I knew they would no longer heed my orders if they sensed any weakness.

It was exhilarating to be in command and using my brain! It seems clear to me now that all young women must have an education and an opportunity to exercise their mental powers through challenging labor. I am determined to raise my daughters to do so, and am resolved to spread this idea of education upon my return home.

©2002 Options Publishing, Inc.

Go on

19 This selection is mostly about

Ⓐ delivering cargo by ship during the 1800s.

Ⓑ a severe storm at sea during the 1800s.

Ⓒ sailing conditions during the 1800s.

Ⓓ a woman learns to navigate a ship during the 1800s.

21 Which of the following details occurs *last* in the journal?

Ⓐ Emma commands the ship through a storm.

Ⓑ Emma befriends the crew.

Ⓒ Emma learns to navigate.

Ⓓ Emma nurses Edward, who has a fever.

20 Which detail *best* supports the main idea of the journal?

Ⓕ The crew is bored and restless.

Ⓖ Two nights ago, I stayed up many hours nursing Edward, who is ill with a fever.

Ⓗ To navigate, or set a course, for the ship, I must learn a great deal of mathematics and trigonometry, which I truly enjoy.

Ⓙ The main mast snapped with a fierce crack as thunder rolled and lightning struck all around us that night.

Clippership *Comet* of New York.

©2002 Options Publishing, Inc.

22 The storm is so violent that Emma worries that waves will wash her overboard; as a result,

    F she ties herself to the bridge.

    G she goes to her cabin.

    H she navigates the ship out of the storm.

    J she has the crew shorten the canvas sails.

23 Which of the following is a *valid* generalization?

    A Women do not possess the same mathematical skills as men.

    B Women make better sea captains than men.

    C Women in the past did not have the same opportunities that they have today.

    D Many women commanded clipper ships and whaling ships.

24 What is the author's purpose in writing this journal?

    F to persuade other women to stitch samplers

    G to describe Emma's experiences and show the importance of education for women

    H to explain how to navigate a ship in the South Pacific

    J to entertain readers with a humorous story about life at sea

25 "The crew is bored and restless. To relieve the *tedium*, the men caught a shark and brought it on board. . . ."
The word *tedium* means

    A excitement.

    B boredom.

    C eagerness.

    D peacefulness.

Stop

©2002 Options Publishing, Inc.

No copying permitted.

Directions

In this part of the test, you will either read or listen to two creation myths: "Why the Fawn Has Spots" and "Pushing Up the Sky." Then you will answer questions to demonstrate how well you understood what you read or how well you listened to what was read to you.

- If this is a Reading Session, your teacher will give you copies of the two creation myths.

- If this is a Listening Session, your teacher will read the selections to you. You will listen to the selections twice. The first time you hear the selections, listen carefully but do not take notes. When you listen to the selections the second time, you will take notes. Use your notes to answer the questions that follow. Use the space below and on the next page for your notes.

Here are some words and definitions you will need to know as you read or listen to the myths:

"Why the Fawn Has Spots"
- **trait:** part of one's character; a quality or characteristic like kindness or selfishness

"Pushing Up the Sky"
- **dissatisfied:** unhappy
- **resolved:** decided

Notes

No copying permitted.

©2002 Options Publishing, Inc.

Notes

Stop

26 Using specific details from the myth, complete the chart below to show what Wakan Takan gave to each animal.

Animal	Gift

27 Explain how the special gifts that Wakan Takan gave to each animal helped it to survive. Use information from the myth to support your answer.

_____

_____

_____

_____

_____

_____

_____

_____

©2002 Options Publishing, Inc.

No copying permitted.

28 What natural event does "Pushing Up the Sky" attempt to explain? Use details from the myth to support your answer.

©2002 Options Publishing, Inc.

No copying permitted.

Planning Page

PLAN your writing for Number 29 here, but do NOT write your final answer on this page. *This page is for your use only. Your writing on this Planning Page will NOT count toward your final score.* Write your final answer on the next page.

©2002 Options Publishing, Inc.

No copying permitted.

29 Discuss why these stories are called creation myths.

In your discussion, be sure to include

- a description of what these myths are called and why
- a comparison of the types of natural events explained
- why you think people told creation myths

 Check your writing for correct spelling, grammar, paragraphs, and punctuation.

_____

_____

_____

_____

_____

_____

_____

_____

_____

_____

_____

_____

_____

_____

_____

_____

_____

_____

_____

Go on

©2002 Options Publishing, Inc.

No copying permitted.

_____

_____

_____

_____

_____

_____

_____

_____

_____

_____

_____

_____

_____

_____

_____

_____

_____

_____

_____

_____

_____

Stop

©2002 Options Publishing, Inc.

No copying permitted.

Directions

In this part of the test, you are going to read an article called "The Italian Granite Worker" and a poem called "Life." First you will answer questions and write about what you have read. You may look back at the article and the poem as often as you like. Then you will be asked to write an essay.

Now begin reading.

The Italian Granite Worker

T his story is based on interviews conducted with Giacomo Coletti as part of the Federal Writers' Project 1936-1940.

The shrill alarm clock breaks the silence of the bleak February morning in 1939. Almost instantly Giacomo Coletti reaches across the bed and turns the alarm off before it wakes his wife, Nina. Dawn has not yet broken, but it is time to get up for work. He begins every morning trying to clear the granite dust that has settled in his throat and lungs.

©2002 Options Publishing, Inc.

No copying permitted.

Giacomo has worked in the granite sheds (the buildings where the stone is cut, carved, and sculpted) since he arrived in the United States from Italy more than 20 years ago. As the years pass, the coughing spells last longer and longer.

Giacomo's eldest son, Giorgio, hears his father's cough. He, like his father, works in the sheds. He worries about his father's health as well as his own. In an attempt to breath as much fresh air as possible, Giorgio sleeps with his windows open even during the harsh New England winters.

Giacomo is well aware of the dangers of working in the granite sheds. Today, they will bury his good friend Pietro. He died of tuberculosis, which is a lung disease. Giacomo recalls with a twinge of guilt the letter he wrote to Pietro, convincing Pietro to leave Italy and join him in Vermont. Pietro was a dear friend. It was Pietro who escorted Giacomo's wife, Nina, across the Atlantic Ocean to the United States.

Nina tries to convince her husband that it is not his fault. She says that it was Pietro's time to die—whether he lived in Italy, Africa, or Montpelier, Vermont.

Giacomo and his Italian, Scottish, Scandinavian, Spanish, and French co-workers will put in a full day's work before they visit Pietro's home. The sheds are grim and gray. Spurts of steam escape from the chimneys. But Giacomo chooses to think of the satisfaction and joy he finds from turning a piece of stone into a beautiful carving.

Inside, Giacomo begins his work. Today, he is carving an angel on a tombstone for a young child who has passed away. He works hard to capture the right look of innocence and joy in the **cherub's** eyes. Giacomo takes special care with this project—he knows the young boy's father.

cherub: an angel usually portrayed as chubby and childlike

At lunchtime, Giacomo and Giorgio make their way home—happy to be free of the **confining** sheds. Nina has prepared their favorite Italian foods for the midday meal. Giacomo and Giorgio also enjoy the many new recipes Nina has learned from her American-born neighbors.

confining: limiting; small and crowded

No copying permitted.

©2002 Options Publishing, Inc.

After work, Giacomo laughs and jokes with his friends. But in the back of his mind, he is thinking about his friend, Pietro, who is not there—the friend he will say good-bye to tonight.

Pietro's home is crowded with granite workers and their families. Eventually the women return home and the men take turns sitting with Pietro. Each time a man coughs or wheezes a tense silence falls on the room. The men wonder to themselves who will be the next to follow Pietro to an early grave.

Years ago, Nina tried to convince Giacomo to find a different line of work. But he never wanted his family to suffer financially. He wanted to feed his children and pay his bills. Giacomo could not take time off to find a new job. Instead, he accepted the fact that the granite dust he breathed in every day might shorten his life. He is too old now to learn a new trade. Besides, he has come to love and appreciate the beauty of granite. Giacomo takes pride in the sculptures he makes. He is proud that his hands create the monuments that keep alive the memory of those, like Pietro, who went before him.

Go on

©2002 Options Publishing Inc.

30 Complete the chart with words or phrases that describe Giacomo Coletti's character. Identify information from the article that supports each character trait.

Character Trait	Supporting Information

31 How does Giacomo Coletti feel about his job in the granite sheds? Explain your answer using details from the article.

_____

_____

_____

_____

_____

_____

_____

_____

_____

_____

©2002 Options Publishing, Inc.

No copying permitted.

Life

Paul Laurence Dunbar

A crust of bread and a corner to sleep in,

A minute to smile and an hour to weep in,

A pint of joy to a peck of trouble,

And never a laugh but the moans come double:

    And that is life!

> **pint of joy to a peck of trouble:** a pint is two cups; a peck is eight quarts or 32 cups

A crust and a corner that love makes precious,

With the smile to warm and the tears to refresh us;

And joys seem sweeter when cares come after,

And a moan is the finest of **foils** for laughter:

    And that is life!

> **foils:** a person or thing that sets off or increases the value of another by contrast; to serve as a contrast to

Go on

©2002 Options Publishing, Inc.

No copying permitted.

32 What is most likely the poet's purpose in writing this poem?
Use ideas from the poem to support your answer.

_____

_____

_____

_____

_____

_____

_____

_____

_____

_____

_____

No copying permitted.

©2002 Options Publishing, Inc.

Planning Page

PLAN your writing for Number 33 here, but do NOT write your final answer on this page. *This page is for your use only. Your writing on this Planning Page will NOT count toward your final score.* Write your final answer beginning on the next page.

Answer

Go on

©2002 Options Publishing, Inc.

No copying permitted.

33 Choose a line or lines from the poem. Discuss the meaning of your selection, and explain how it applies to Giacomo Coletti. Use ideas from BOTH the poem and the article in your answer.

In your answer, be sure to include

- the line or lines you have selected from the poem
- an explanation of how your selection applies to Giacomo Coletti

Check your writing for correct spelling, grammar, paragraphs, and punctuation.

_____

_____

_____

_____

_____

_____

_____

_____

_____

_____

_____

_____

_____

_____

_____

_____

_____

_____

_____

_____

©2002 Options Publishing, Inc.

No copying permitted.

©2002 Options Publishing, Inc.

Go on

Planning Page

PLAN your writing for Number 34 here, but do NOT write your final answer on this page. *This page is for your use only. Your writing on this Planning Page will NOT count toward your final score.* Write your final answer beginning on the next page.

©2002 Options Publishing, Inc.

No copying permitted.

34 Both "An Italian Granite Worker" and "Life" describe life as a mixture of hard times and good times. Write an essay about a person in history or someone *you* know who has experienced difficult times but still appreciates life and takes pride in his or her accomplishments.

In your essay, be sure to include

- who the person is
- what he or she did
- the difficulties he or she faced
- why the person takes pride in his or her accomplishments
- an introduction, a body, and a conclusion

Check your writing for correct spelling, grammar, paragraphs, and punctuation.

_____

_____

_____

_____

_____

_____

_____

_____

_____

_____

_____

_____

_____

_____

©2002 Options Publishing, Inc.

Go on

_____

_____

_____

_____

_____

_____

_____

_____

_____

_____

_____

_____

_____

_____

_____

_____

_____

_____

_____

_____

_____

You have now completed TEST A. Your teacher will help you score your test.

Stop

©2002 Options Publishing, Inc.

No copying permitted.

Directions for Reading Session

In this part of the test, you will read two articles and a story, and answer questions about what you have read. You may look back at the selections as often as you like.

Now begin reading.

TEST B

Reading Session

Directions

Here is the article about Ernest Shackleton and his expedition to Antarctica. Read "Stranded in Antarctica." Then answer Numbers 1 through 8.

STRANDED IN ANTARCTICA

Abandon ship!" Shackleton shouted out. It was October 27, 1915, and with this command, Ernest Shackleton knew he had also abandoned his dream to be the first to walk across the continent of Antarctica. He also knew that survival on the frozen sea was almost impossible. It was 1915, and there were no radios, telephones, or high-tech tools for navigation. The crew scrambled to get food, gear, and the lifeboats off the ship. They would need these small boats if they hoped to survive.

◆　◆　◆

A year earlier, Shackleton's trip began well enough. The British eagerly supported and financed the expedition. Yet Shackleton knew it would not be an easy trip. In Antarctica, the winter temperature can drop to 100° below zero Fahrenheit as winter winds race across the ice at 200 miles per hour. Shackleton hired an experienced crew and planned the expedition for the spring, when weather conditions were a little better.

On August 1, 1914, *Endurance* and its crew left the dock in London, and by October they arrived in Buenos Aires, on the coast of Argentina. Here, they picked up the sled dogs, and on November 5, the ship landed at the whaling town on South Georgia Island, located southeast off the tip of South America. Because the seasons are reversed in the Southern Hemisphere, spring was under way. The plan was to leave immediately for Antarctica; however, a severe, brutal winter delayed the voyage. Ice still

The *Endurance* trapped in the ice pack.

©2002 Options Publishing, Inc.

No copying permitted.

Shackleton and the crew dragging a lifeboat across the ice.

choked most of the Weddell Sea, just north of Antarctica. Another tedious month passed until, finally, on December 5, *Endurance* set sail for the southern continent.

The men had never seen so much ice, and they lost precious months picking their way through icebergs. By January 19, 1915, the ship was still 100 miles from the continent, but the frozen Weddell Sea surrounded *Endurance* on all sides, and the ice pack was drifting northward, taking the ship with it.

Shackleton soon realized that they would spend the winter trapped on the ship. Howling blizzards overwhelmed the men as they worked day and night chipping away at the ice crushing the ship. It was a hopeless battle—the boards on deck twisted, and the ship's hull sprang leaks. Shackleton wrote in his diary, "It was a sickening sensation to feel the decks breaking up under one's feet, the great beams bending and then snapping with a noise like gun-fire." On October 27, 1915, Shackleton ordered the crew to abandon the ship. Soon after, the ice crushed *Endurance* and it sank. Now the men and their supplies stood on the frozen sea; however, it was spring in Antarctica, and the shifting ice pack could suddenly break apart under their feet. If the men did not move soon, none would survive.

Shackleton and the men decided to haul the supplies and lifeboats across the frozen sea to Paulet Island, 346 miles to the northwest. Dragging the boats was grueling. The ice was in jagged pieces, and the men often had to lift the boats over waves frozen in midair. But the boats were necessary. Soon, the crew hoped, they would reach open water—and home.

©2002 Options Publishing, Inc.

 No copying permitted.

Shackleton's challenge was to hold the twenty-seven men together—without one another, they would all die. They must make open water before the soft ice crumbled beneath them. Finally, on March 9, 1916, the men felt the swell of the ocean beneath the ice pack. They were 30 miles from the open ocean. A month later, the sea opened, and Shackleton gave orders to launch the boats. The voyagers had marched 600 backbreaking miles since the ice first trapped *Endurance*. They had risked starvation, drowning, and freezing to death.

The men rowed with all their remaining strength, struggling to avoid icebergs. As night came, the exhausted crew looked for a firm ice pack to camp. Fortunately, apprehension kept Shackleton awake. During the night, he left his tent and watched in horror as the ice pack suddenly cracked under the men's tent! The men quickly pulled one another from the tent.

"Launch the boats!" Shackleton yelled. Men grabbed instruments, gear, and food as they tried to outrun the cracking ice. Once in the boats, Frank Worsley, the navigator and captain, set a course to Elephant Island.

On April 15, the half-frozen men landed on Elephant Island—solid land at last! Yet they knew they could not survive the winter on this barren, wind-blown island. Someone had to get help—and that help was at the whaling town on South Georgia Island, 800 miles to the east. Nine days later, Shackleton and five of the crew took a lifeboat and set off. It was a miserable journey as terrifying gales blew the ship off course and waves soaked the men. Subzero temperatures froze their clothing. Sleep was impossible. Everyone suffered from frostbite. Seventeen agonizing days later, the men landed on the island, but they had one last ordeal to overcome. The whaling town was on the other side of the island, and *no one* had ever crossed the island's mountain range. It was a tremendous risk, but Shackleton knew it was his only hope of saving the men.

On May 18, Shackleton and two of the crew set off. Exhausted, they reached the summit and pressed on. Finally, they saw the town before them. As they staggered into the factory manager's house, they knew the rescue of the entire crew was now certain.

Unbelievably, Shackleton and the crew of twenty-seven men all lived. With Shackleton's leadership, they managed to survive by using courage, strength, and teamwork.

Go on

1 What is the author's purpose in writing this article?

Ⓐ to entertain readers with an amusing story

Ⓑ to explain how and why the *Endurance* sank

Ⓒ to describe how Shackleton and the men survived being stranded in Antarctica

Ⓓ to persuade others to explore the South Pole

2 "Stranded in Antarctica" is an article because it is a work of

Ⓕ nonfiction that tries to persuade a reader to think a certain way.

Ⓖ fiction that has characters and events that are not real.

Ⓗ nonfiction that is written by a person about his or her own life.

Ⓙ nonfiction that gives the reader facts about a subject.

3 You can draw the conclusion that the members of the crew most likely

Ⓐ were unhappy with Shackleton's leadership.

Ⓑ were experienced sailors.

Ⓒ looked forward to the challenge of rowing to Paulet Island.

Ⓓ were surprised that Shackleton returned to rescue them from Elephant Island.

4 In 1914, the expedition had to wait an extra month at South Georgia Island before leaving for the Antarctic because the winter was so severe. You can infer that the winter of 1914 was unusually harsh because

Ⓕ they enjoyed their stopover at South Georgia Island and decided to stay longer.

Ⓖ the expedition had to wait for the sled dogs to arrive.

Ⓗ Shackleton would not have left if he thought the ship would become trapped in ice.

Ⓙ the seasons are reversed in the Southern Hemisphere.

5 How many miles did the men have to row from Elephant Island to reach South Georgia Island?

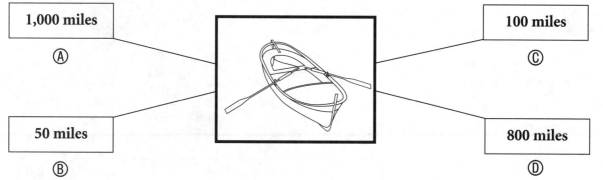

1,000 miles
Ⓐ

50 miles
Ⓑ

100 miles
Ⓒ

800 miles
Ⓓ

No copying permitted.

©2002 Options Publishing, Inc.

6 Which of the following statements is a *valid* generalization?

   Ⓕ Shackleton showed strong leadership qualities throughout the expedition.

   Ⓖ All the crew of *Endurance* respected Shackleton.

   Ⓗ Sailing for hours on the ocean is a boring task.

   Ⓙ Anyone can become a member of a wilderness expedition.

8 The passage states that "a *severe*, brutal winter delayed the voyage." In this context, the word *severe* means

   Ⓕ pleasant.

   Ⓖ harsh.

   Ⓗ scorching.

   Ⓙ strict.

7 Which of the following statements is an opinion?

   Ⓐ The men thought the sight of land was beautiful.

   Ⓑ All twenty-seven men survived the expedition to Antarctica.

   Ⓒ The ship *Endurance* was crushed by an ice pack.

   Ⓓ Winter temperatures in Antarctica can drop to 100° F. below zero.

Go on

©2002 Options Publishing, Inc.

Directions

Here is an article about a tragic fire that occurred in Colorado. Read "Trapped in a Firestorm." Then answer Numbers 9 through 18.

Trapped in a Firestorm

A view of Storm King Mountain after the fire.

On Storm King Mountain near Glenwood Springs, Colorado, fourteen white crosses stand among blackened trees. The crosses mark where firefighters fell during the worst United States wildfire disaster in modern history. With binoculars, Chuck Johnson can see the crosses from his back porch. "I think about the fire every time I look up there. And every time, I feel a sense of sadness."

In the summer of 1994, after an unusually hot and dry spring, weather forecasters predicted a high risk for fire. Their predictions came true. By late June, wildfires were burning across Colorado and the West, and resources to fight them were running low. Storm King was covered with tall oak trees, pinion-juniper trees, and dead brush. When a severe lightning storm struck the mountain on July 2, a fire ignited. For two days, fire officials debated who should battle the blaze, yet no one hiked to the fire to assess the danger.

Residents nearby grew angry as they watched the fire spread. They feared the blaze would reach their homes, and they questioned why Storm King was not a high priority. On July 5, the Bureau of Land Management (BLM) sent a small crew up the mountain. It was a difficult climb, as the crew slipped on loose rocks, ran into near-vertical drop-offs, and got tangled in a maze of tree branches. By afternoon the firefighters had cleared a helicopter-landing site and started a fire line encircling the burning area. But after both of their chain saws broke, they called it quits and headed down the mountain. Meanwhile, an air tanker flew over the fire, dropping retardant. The pilot made two passes, and then decided that a helicopter with a water bucket could do a better job. He turned back for home.

©2002 Options Publishing, Inc.

No copying permitted.

That night eight **smoke jumpers** parachuted onto Storm King. They hiked to the helicopter-landing site and saw that flames had spread across the fire line. With their headlamps on, they worked in the opposite direction, down the eastern slope. The terrain was steeper and rockier than they expected. In darkness it became too dangerous to stay on the rough slope, so they went back to the helicopter site and camped. A cool breeze blew over the mountaintop, and the crew sensed the weather was changing.

The next morning a cold front moved quickly toward Storm King. Forecasters issued a red flag warning for high, gusty winds, a serious alert for firefighters. But the smoke jumpers atop the mountain never received this warning. They had watched the fire grow overnight and knew they needed more help to bring it under control. They radioed for helicopters and two more crews, Hotshots if possible. Hotshots, a specially trained team, go where needed to fight fires.

Don Mackey, the smoke jumper in charge, learned that only one helicopter and one crew of Hotshots was available. Eight more smoke jumpers would also join the fight, along with a bigger BLM crew. The fire covered more than 125 acres. The team split into groups. Mackey led one group downhill—confident his plan for the fire could work, if the wind held off. The crew worked blindly in the summer heat. Dense vegetation and a small ridge blocked their view below. Even worse, their lookouts on the ridge could not see Mackey's team. The lookouts worried about the fighters' safety. In late afternoon, from atop the ridge, a column of smoke was spotted. The helicopter flew toward the area to drop water, but then the winds suddenly picked up. The new fire was rapidly spreading, and no amount of water could stop it. In a matter of minutes, swirling winds created an enormous firestorm that raced toward the firefighters on the slope. It moved faster than any human could run. Those who were closest to the ridge top survived. The other fourteen men and women, including Mackey, died where the flames overtook them.

An investigation of the incident blamed poor communication, a disregard for safety rules, and the "can-do" attitude of the firefighters for the Storm King tragedy.

> **smoke jumpers:**
> forest firefighters who parachute into locations that are difficult to reach

A smoke jumper practices a landing.

Go on

©2002 Options Publishing, Inc.

9 This article is mostly about

Ⓐ the dangers of fighting wildfires.

Ⓑ 14 firefighters fought the fire on the mountain.

Ⓒ how Hotshots and smoke jumpers fight fires.

Ⓓ mistakes in judgment caused 14 deaths during a wildfire on Storm King Mountain.

10 Which detail from the article *best* supports the author's main idea?

Ⓕ The BLM thought the fire would burn itself out.

Ⓖ Fire crews had difficulty climbing the rocky mountain.

Ⓗ The fire was not a priority, and officials could not agree on who should fight it.

Ⓙ An air tanker flew over the fire and dropped retardant.

11 The firefighters on the side of the mountain died because

Ⓐ they were not the fastest runners.

Ⓑ they were too far down the slope and could not outrun the fire.

Ⓒ tree branches blocked their escape route.

Ⓓ strong winds made it difficult for them to run fast.

12 Why did the lookouts worry about the firefighters' safety?

Ⓕ If a fire started nearby, the firefighters might not see it and might become trapped.

Ⓖ They knew one helicopter was not enough to help them.

Ⓗ Their chain saws kept breaking.

Ⓙ They lost radio contact with their lookouts.

Another view of Storm King Mountain.

©2002 Options Publishing, Inc.

No copying permitted.

13 You can infer that if the fire crews had received the red flag warning,

Ⓐ their plan of attack would have been different.

Ⓑ more water drops would have been ordered.

Ⓒ they would have called for weather updates.

Ⓓ they would have worked in larger groups.

14 Where is Storm King Mountain located?

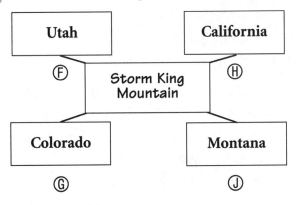

15 Who arrived *first* on the mountain to fight the fire?

Ⓐ the smoke jumpers

Ⓑ residents who lived near the mountain

Ⓒ the BLM crew

Ⓓ the Hotshots

16 Which of the following statements is a fact?

Ⓕ Hotshots are better trained than smoke jumpers.

Ⓖ Don Mackey loved his job.

Ⓗ The fire on Storm King was an awesome sight.

Ⓙ Hot, dry weather conditions put Storm King at high risk for fire.

17 "Trapped in a Firestorm" is a work of nonfiction because it

Ⓐ gives information about real people, places, or events.

Ⓑ develops fictional characters and events.

Ⓒ is passed down orally from one generation to the next.

Ⓓ teaches the reader a lesson about life.

18 "The *terrain* was steeper and rockier than they expected. In the darkness, it became too dangerous to stay on the rough slope." The word *terrain* means

Ⓕ fire.

Ⓖ river.

Ⓗ neighborhood.

Ⓙ land.

Go on

©2002 Options Publishing, Inc.

No copying permitted.

Directions

Here is the story that presents you with a very puzzling problem. Read "The Lady or the Tiger?" Then answer Numbers 19 through 25.

The Lady or the Tiger?

by Frank R. Stockton

Long ago, there lived a savage, cruel king, who believed that he was a brilliant and reasonable sovereign. He also believed that justice was best served in his arena, for he felt it improved the minds of his subjects. In this arena, crime was punished and virtue was rewarded without the aid of judges or juries. A person's guilt or innocence was decided by mere chance. When a subject was accused of a crime, public notice was given that on an appointed day the fate of the accused would be determined in the king's arena.

On the appointed day, the king gave a signal and the accused stepped out into the arena. Directly opposite him were two identical doors. It was the duty of the subject to open one—he could open either door. From one, a ferocious tiger might spring upon him as a punishment for his guilt. From the other, a beautiful lady might step out and, as a reward of his innocence, immediately marry the man. It was of no consequence that he might already be wed. The king permitted no such arrangements to interfere with his magnificent plan of punishment and reward.

This merciless king had a beautiful daughter—but she was as arrogant and proud as her father was. Among the king's servants was a handsome young man. It was not long before the princess fell deeply in love with him. They met for many months until, one day, the king learned of their love. He immediately threw the young servant into prison and set a day for his trial.

©2002 Options Publishing, Inc.

The king chose a most savage tiger to crouch behind one door and a beautiful servant girl to stand behind the other. The young man would die or marry—in either case, the king was rid of him. The trial day arrived, and the king gave the signal. The young man walked into the arena and bowed to the king, but the youth's eyes were fixed upon the princess.

From the moment of his arrest, the princess thought of nothing but this hour. For she had done what no other person had done—she had discovered the secret behind the doors. She knew behind which door the tiger paced and behind which the lady waited. The princess was familiar with the lady, who was one of the fairest and loveliest of the court—and the princess hated her. Often the princess had seen, or imagined that she had seen, the lady look with affection upon the young man, and the princess feared that the young man returned this look to the lady. Occasionally, the princess had seen them talking together—just for a moment or two—but the princess was jealous.

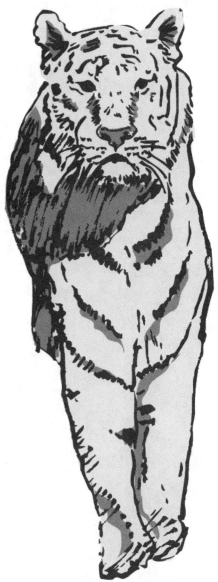

As the young man looked at the princess, he could tell she knew the secret. He had expected her to know, for she was his only hope. As their eyes met, the princess knew his question: "Which?" There was not an instant to be lost. The question was asked in a flash; it must be answered in another. She raised her hand, and made a slight, quick movement toward the right. No one but the young man saw it, and he walked rapidly across the empty space. He went directly to the door on the right and opened it.

Now, the point of the story is this: Did the tiger come out of that door, or did the lady?

The answer involves a study of the human heart. She had lost him, but who should have him? Often she cried out as she imagined her lover opening the door to meet the cruel fangs of the tiger! But how much oftener she imagined him opening the other door. Oh, how it páined her when she saw his look of delight as he met the lady! Her thoughts tortured her. She knew the young man would ask her, and she knew she would answer. And without the slightest hesitation, she had moved her hand to the right.

So, fair reader, which came out of the opened door—the lady or the tiger?

©2002 Options Publishing, Inc.

Go on

19 Which statement *best* describes the main idea of this story?

Ⓐ The reader is challenged to guess the princess's decision.

Ⓑ Justice was not always fair in ancient times.

Ⓒ Fierce tigers were used in the king's arena.

Ⓓ The king was very cruel.

20 Which detail from the story *best* supports the main idea?

Ⓕ "A person's guilt or innocence was decided by mere chance."

Ⓖ "This merciless king had a beautiful daughter . . ."

Ⓗ "The king chose a most savage tiger to crouch behind one door . . ."

Ⓙ "The answer involves a study of the human heart."

21 Which event happens *first* in the plot of the story?

Ⓐ The king throws the young man into prison.

Ⓑ The young man opens the door.

Ⓒ The king discovers that the princess loves the young man.

Ⓓ The princess discovers the secret behind the doors.

No copying permitted.

©2002 Options Publishing, Inc.

22 The princess could save the young man's life because

- (F) the princess could beg her father to save the young man.
- (G) he knew that she loved him.
- (H) she knew behind which door the tiger sat.
- (J) the princess knew he loved the lady behind the door.

23 Which of the following statements is a *valid* generalization?

- (A) All the people enjoyed attending the event in the king's arena.
- (B) Princesses are proud and cruel.
- (C) The king always based his idea of justice on chance.
- (D) Most of the accused people in the king's arena were guilty.

24 What is the author's purpose in writing this story?

- (F) to describe a question that makes readers think about human nature
- (G) to entertain readers with a humorous and amusing story
- (H) to persuade readers that life in ancient times was often cruel and unfair
- (J) to explain how the king administered justice

25 "[The princess] was as *arrogant* and proud as her father was." The word *arrogant* means

- (A) violent.
- (B) conceited.
- (C) humble.
- (D) modest.

Stop

©2002 Options Publishing, Inc.

Directions

In this part of the test, you will either read or listen to an article called "Christmas Eve Escape" and a letter written by Frederick Douglass called "Letter to Harriet Tubman." Then you will answer questions to demonstrate how well you understood what you read or how well you listened to what was read to you.

- If this is a Reading Session, your teacher will give you copies of the two selections.

- If this is a Listening Session, your teacher will read the selections to you. You will listen to the selections twice. The first time you hear the selections, listen carefully but do not take notes. When you listen to the selections the second time, you will take notes. Use your notes to answer the questions that follow. Use the space below and on the next page for your notes.

Here are the words and definitions you will need to know as you read or listen to "Letter to Harriet Tubman":

- **marked:** noticeably
- **wrought:** worked
- **multitude:** crowd of people

Notes

©2002 Options Publishing, Inc.

No copying permitted.

Notes

Frederick Douglass

©2002 Options Publishing, Inc.

Stop

26 Using specific details from the article, complete the chart below to compare Harriet Tubman with Moses.

Harriet Tubman	Moses

27 Why do you think it was so important to Harriet Tubman to devote her life to running the Underground Railroad? Use information from the article to support your answer.

_____

_____

_____

_____

_____

_____

_____

_____

©2002 Options Publishing, Inc.

No copying permitted.

28 What does Douglass try to explain in his letter to Harriet Tubman?
Use details from the letter to support your answer.

_____

_____

_____

_____

_____

_____

_____

_____

_____

_____

_____

_____

_____

_____

_____

_____

Go on

©2002 Options Publishing, Inc.

Planning Page

PLAN your writing for Number 29 here, but do NOT write your final answer on this page. *This page is for your use only. Your writing on this Planning Page will NOT count toward your final score.* Write your final answer beginning on the next page.

©2002 Options Publishing, Inc.

No copying permitted.

29 From what you have learned in these two selections, compare and contrast the lives of Frederick Douglass and Harriet Tubman.

In your discussion, be sure to include

- a comparison of the work that each person did
- a contrast of their work
- what you can infer about Douglass's feelings toward Harriet Tubman

 Check your writing for correct spelling, grammar, paragraphs, and punctuation.

Go on

©2002 Options Publishing, Inc.

Stop

No copying permitted.

©2002 Options Publishing, Inc.

Directions

In this part of the test, you are going to read an article called "The Fight for Equality" and a poem called "See It Through." First you will answer questions and write about what you have read. You may look back at the article and the poem as often as you like. Then you will be asked to write an essay.

Now begin reading.

The Fight for Equality

It is Election Day in Rochester, New York. The polls are open and United States citizens stand in line to vote for the next president of the United States. Among those in line are sixteen women voting for the first time. They cast their ballots and leave the polling place. Three weeks later, all sixteen women are arrested.

The women, led by Susan B. Anthony, were all citizens of the United States, but the year was 1872. Women could not legally vote.

In 1868, the Fourteenth Amendment to the Constitution was passed. It stated that all people born in the United States were citizens and that no citizen could be denied legal privileges. Anthony and several other women thought it was time to put this law to a test by voting. They felt they deserved the same civil and political rights as American men. Anthony, the most famous and outspoken, was the only one in the group that was ordered to stand trial.

While awaiting her trial, Anthony traveled across the country speaking out against the way women were viewed and treated in American society. Finally, on June 17, 1873, Anthony did stand trial. But the judge, who opposed women's suffrage, made his decision before the trial even began. He did not allow Anthony to testify on her own behalf. He ordered the jury to find her guilty of violating voting laws. He also fined her $100—a fee she refused to pay and remains unpaid to this day. Anthony knew that if she were put in prison for not paying the

Susan B. Anthony

©2002 Options Publishing, Inc.

fine, she would be able to test the law by having a new trial. The judge also knew this, and he did not imprison her for failing to pay the fine. This denied her the chance to appeal the court's decision and challenge the Fourteenth Amendment.

Anthony's brush with the law did not discourage her from continuing the campaign for equality. In fact, little in her life had ever discouraged this determined woman. Born to Quaker parents in 1820, Anthony experienced freedom and respect that many other girls were denied growing up in the United States. Quakers were among the first groups to practice full equality for the sexes and the races. Anthony's parents were strong supporters of the temperance (avoidance of alcohol) and the abolitionist (antislavery) movements. Quakers believed that slavery was morally wrong. They helped to organize and operate the Underground Railroad, which helped slaves escape to Canada. In her parents' home, Anthony learned independence, courage, and a passion for justice. Everyone in the Anthony home was dedicated to the movement to end slavery. It was the abolitionists and their actions who forced the nation to deal with the issue of slavery.

At seventeen, Anthony finished school and took her first paying job as a teacher, where her salary was about one-fifth of what male teachers made. Anthony thought this was unfair. When she protested and asked for equal pay, she lost her job. She found another teaching position. And she continued the fight to free all slaves immediately.

At an antislavery meeting in 1851, she met a woman who became a life-long friend and political partner—Elizabeth Cady Stanton. The two also supported temperance—laws that prohibit the sale of alcohol. They spoke out against the abuse of women and children by men who were alcoholics. At a temperance meeting, Anthony was not allowed to speak because she was a woman. She was told by the men to "listen and learn." In Anthony's upbringing, everyone in the family was allowed to express an opinion. It was after that meeting that

©2002 Options Publishing, Inc.

No copying permitted.

she vowed to join Stanton and dedicate herself to gaining rights for women. Despite the horrible and unjust things said about her in the newspapers, Anthony continued to travel and make public speeches supporting women's rights.

In 1866, Anthony and Stanton founded the American Equal Rights Association. Three years later, a large portion of the group broke away to form their own group called the American Woman Suffrage Association. The main difference between the groups was their approach to achieving the vote. Stanton and Anthony wanted to gain the vote for women at the national level. The new group wanted to gain the vote on a state-by-state basis.

Anthony worked for women's rights up until the day she died—March 13, 1906. When she died, women could vote in only four states—Wyoming, Colorado, Idaho, and Utah.

On June 4, 1919, fourteen years after Anthony's death, the Nineteenth Amendment was passed, giving women the right to vote.

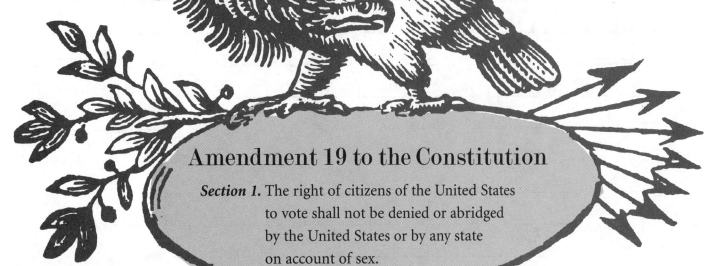

Amendment 19 to the Constitution

Section 1. The right of citizens of the United States to vote shall not be denied or abridged by the United States or by any state on account of sex.

Go on

©2002 Options Publishing, Inc.

No copying permitted.

30 Complete the chart with words or phrases that describe Susan B. Anthony's character. Identify information from the article that supports each character trait.

Character Traits	Supporting Information

31 How did Anthony feel about slavery and the use of alcohol? Explain your answer using details from the article.

_____

_____

_____

_____

_____

_____

_____

_____

_____

©2002 Options Publishing, Inc.

No copying permitted.

See It Through

Edgar A. Guest

When you're up against a trouble,
Meet it squarely, face to face;
Lift your chin and set your shoulders,
Plant your feet and take a brace.
When it's **vain** to try to dodge it,
Do the best that you can do;
You may fail, but you may conquer,
See it through!

> **vain:** unsuccessful; useless

Black may be the clouds about you
And your future may seem **grim**,
But don't let your nerve desert you;
Keep yourself in fighting trim.
If the worst is bound to happen,
Spite of all that you can do,
Running from it will not save you,
See it through!

> **grim:** cheerless

Even hope may seem but **futile**,
When with troubles you're **beset**,
But remember you are facing
Just what other men have met.
You may fail, but fall still fighting;
Don't give up, whate'er you do;
Eyes front, head high to the finish.
See it through!

> **futile:** useless

> **beset:** attacked on all sides

©2002 Options Publishing, Inc.

Go on

32 What is most likely the poet's main purpose in writing this poem?
Use ideas from the poem to support your answer.

_____

_____

_____

_____

_____

_____

_____

_____

_____

_____

_____

_____

_____

_____

No copying permitted.

©2002 Options Publishing, Inc.

Planning Page

PLAN your writing for Number 33 here, but do NOT write your final answer on this page. *This page is for your use only. Your writing on this Planning Page will NOT count toward your final score.* Write your final answer beginning on the next page.

Answer

©2002 Options Publishing, Inc.

No copying permitted.

33 Choose a line or lines from the poem. Discuss the meaning of your selection, and explain how it applies to Susan B. Anthony. Use ideas from BOTH the poem and the article in your answer.

In your answer, be sure to include
- the line or lines you have selected from the poem
- an explanation of how your selection applies to Susan B. Anthony

Check your writing for correct spelling, grammar, paragraphs, and punctuation.

_____

_____

_____

_____

_____

_____

_____

_____

_____

_____

_____

_____

_____

_____

_____

_____

_____

©2002 Options Publishing, Inc.

_____

_____

_____

_____

_____

_____

_____

_____

_____

_____

_____

_____

_____

_____

_____

_____

_____

_____

_____

_____

_____

_____

_____

_____

Go on

©2002 Options Publishing, Inc.

Planning Page

PLAN your writing for Number 34 here, but do NOT write your final answer on this page. *This page is for your use only. Your writing on this Planning Page will NOT count toward your final score.* Write your final answer beginning on the next page.

No copying permitted.

©2002 Options Publishing, Inc.

34 Write an essay about a person in history or someone *you* know who has overcome obstacles to achieve an important goal.

In your essay, be sure to include

- who the person is
- what he or she did
- the difficulties he or she faced
- how the difficulties were overcome
- an introduction, a body, and a conclusion

Check your writing for correct spelling, grammar, paragraphs, and punctuation.

_____

_____

_____

_____

_____

_____

_____

_____

_____

_____

_____

_____

_____

_____

_____

_____

_____

©2002 Options Publishing, Inc.

Go on

_____

_____

_____

_____

_____

_____

_____

_____

_____

_____

_____

_____

_____

_____

_____

_____

_____

_____

_____

_____

_____

_____

_____

_____

You have now completed TEST B. Your teacher will help you score your test.

Stop

No copying permitted.

©2002 Options Publishing, Inc.

Y ou have already completed Test A on pages 3 through 34. The following pages reproduce Test A, but this time you will learn why specific multiple-choice answers are correct or incorrect. You will also learn how to become a better listener and writer.

By reading these pages and completing the exercises, you will learn strategies that will help you take tests, understand what you hear, and improve your writing skills.

The following test will help you master important reading, thinking, and writing skills:

- **Reading Session:** Each multiple-choice question is labeled with the *type* of skill it teaches. You will also learn how to choose the correct answer by reading why each answer is correct or incorrect. You will learn **Strategies and Tips** for answering the questions. And you will practice what you have learned about each skill with a **TRY IT!** activity.

- **Reading and Listening Session:** In this part of the test, you read two selections or listened as your teacher read the two selections aloud to you. On the following pages, you will learn how to take notes about the most important details and ideas in the selections. You will also learn how to understand and explain those important ideas by organizing your thoughts *before* you write your answers. By using the **Strategies and Tips** in this part of the test, you will learn how to become a better listener, reader, note-taker, and writer. Use the **TRY IT!** activities to practice the skills you have learned.

- **Writing Session:** In this part of the test, you will learn **Strategies and Tips** for finding supporting details, understanding diagrams, and organizing your writing by using an outline. Use the **TRY IT!** activities to sharpen your thinking and writing skills.

Directions for Reading Session

In this part of the test, you will read a story, an article, and a journal. As you answer the questions about what you have read, you may look back at the reading selections as often as you like.

Now begin reading.

©2002 Options Publishing, Inc.

Directions

Here is the story "The Fortune Cookie" that appeared in Test A. Reread the story, and then compare *your* answers with the answers given here. Read *Strategies and Tips* to learn how to find the correct answers, and use the *TRY IT!* activities for additional practice.

THE FORTUNE COOKIE

"Let me read mine now, Mom!" cried Quan, pushing away his empty plate. "'A stitch in time saves nine.'"

"That's easy," laughed Mrs. Li. "If you do your homework as soon as it's assigned, it will save you a lot of worry in the future. Min, what words of advice does yours give?"

Min looked around the circle of happy faces at the table. It was a family tradition to celebrate birthdays at the local Chinese Restaurant, and today she was thirteen years old. The climax of the meal was the sharing of their fortune cookies, and the linen cloth was littered with crumbs and the discarded words of wisdom. "No, I want to keep mine until I have figured out what it means for myself," Min said. She placed the slip of paper carefully in her purse. Min had the feeling that it meant something special.

The following day was Saturday. "No school," Min said happily to herself, as she curled her toes under the blanket. The sun was shining through the windows and she, Carol, and her friends had planned a picnic down in the park. The whole day seemed to stretch invitingly before her.

"Min, are you awake?" Her mother's voice roused her from her daydreams. "Get up, hon, I want you to go on an errand for me."

"Oh Mom, what is it?" Reluctantly Min dragged herself into the kitchen.

"Do me a favor and take these groceries across to Mrs. Spencer. She has hurt her back and is having difficulty going to the stores right now." Min pulled on jeans and a T-shirt, ran a comb through her short dark hair, picked up the groceries, and dashed across the street. She knocked impatiently on her neighbor's back door and went in—not waiting to be invited.

©2002 Options Publishing, Inc.

No copying permitted.

However, as she placed the brown paper bag on the kitchen table, something prompted her to put her head around the living room door. The drapes were still closed, and the room was in darkness. Min padded across to the hallway and called gently, "Mrs. Spencer, it's Min. Mom sent over some groceries."

A faint voice answered from a bedroom upstairs. "Thank you, Min. Please excuse me if I don't come down to greet you."

"Mrs. Spencer, are you all right? May I come up?"

From the bedroom doorway, Min smiled shyly at her silver-haired neighbor. She looked frailer and more fragile than Min remembered her. "Mrs. Spencer, you don't look well. Can I fix you some breakfast?" She could see from the look of relief on Mrs. Spencer's face that this was a very welcome offer. "Oh well," Min thought, "Carol would wait for half an hour."

Min carried the tray of eggs, toast, and coffee upstairs, intending to leave it and scoot home, but on an impulse, or whim, she found herself asking, "Mrs. Spencer, would you like me to collect your mail?" Minutes later she had plumped up the pillows and made Mrs. Spencer comfortable with the tray. As Min put the letters and newspaper next to Mrs. Spencer, it struck her that something was not quite right. "Mrs. Spencer, where are your reading glasses?"

"I'm afraid I broke them, dear, when I fell. I do feel so helpless without them."

Hours later, when Mrs. Li came across to see what had happened to her daughter, she found Min and Mrs. Spencer curled up together on the bed, deep in conversation. Opened letters and discarded newspapers lay beside them.

"It was really sweet of you to give up your day to help Mrs. Spencer," Min's mother said as they made their way across the street. "Carol called to say that they couldn't wait for you any longer."

"It's all right, Mom. I guess I understand my fortune cookie now." Min smiled as she took it out of her purse and put it on the dressing table. She recited it quietly to herself: "The more you give away, the more you have."

©2002 Options Publishing, Inc.

Go on

Question 1   This question is about **identifying the author's purpose** for writing. The *author's purpose* is the reason he or she wrote the selection.

Strategies and Tips for Identifying the Author's Purpose

An author usually has two purposes for writing—a **general purpose** and a **specific purpose**. Knowing an author's purpose helps you judge the writer and the selection fairly.

- The **general purpose** might be to entertain, to persuade, to inform, to explain, or to describe. "The Fortune Cookie" *explains* an experience Min had that changed the way she thought about life.
- The **specific purpose** is tied to the theme of the story and is the main point the author wants to make about the topic. Often, the author reinforces the specific purpose in the closing paragraph of the article. The theme is expressed by the message in the fortune cookie: "The more you give away, the more you have." The more goodness and kindness you give to others, the more goodness and kindness you have in yourself.

1 **What is the author's general purpose in writing this article?**

Ⓐ to entertain readers with an amusing story

Incorrect. The author wants to do more than entertain you. The writer wants to explain how an experience can change the way you think about life.

Ⓑ to explain how an experience can change a person's outlook on life

Correct. This is the *author's general purpose*. The story is about a life-changing experience the main character has.

Ⓒ to describe how plans for a day can quickly change

Incorrect. This is not the author's purpose. This is just one of the results that occurs when Min decides to stay with her neighbor.

Ⓓ to persuade readers to take groceries to their neighbors

Incorrect. The author is not trying to persuade readers to take groceries to their neighbors. This is a detail. The author's purpose is to explain a life-changing experience.

TRY IT! To help identify the author's purpose for writing, answer the following questions.

1. What specific, or main, point does the author want to communicate?

_____

_____

2. How does the author want me to respond after reading this story?

_____

_____

©2002 Options Publishing, Inc.

No copying permitted.

Question 2   This question is about **identifying the genre** of a selection. The *genre* identifies the type of literary work, such as nonfiction, fiction, poetry, and drama. Each genre has its own unique characteristics.

Strategies and Tips for Identifying Genre

Literary **genre** refers to the type of literature you read.

- **Fiction** is writing that uses characters and events that are not real. Myths, folktales, and many short stories are fiction.

- The genre, or type of literary work, called **realistic fiction** consists of stories about characters that are set in modern times and that have events that are realistic—they could happen. The stories help us understand ourselves and others by showing that people have problems, feelings, experiences, and thoughts similar to our own. The plots in realistic fiction are true-to-life portrayals of events. In other words, the characters seem real, and the events could have happened. "The Fortune Cookie" is realistic fiction.

- **Nonfiction** is writing that uses people, places, and events that are real. Articles, essays, biographies, autobiographies, and profiles are all nonfiction. They are about real people, places, or events.

2   "The Fortune Cookie" can best be described as a work

Ⓕ of nonfiction that gives the reader facts about a subject.

Incorrect. This story is fiction and does not give you facts about a specific topic.

Ⓖ of fiction, but the characters seem real, and the events could have happened.

Correct. This is a description of realistic fiction. Although the characters are fictional and events did not really happen, they are realistic. They could have happened.

Ⓗ of nonfiction that tries to persuade a reader to think a certain way.

Incorrect. An essay typically tries to persuade a reader to act or think a certain way.

Ⓙ of nonfiction that gives facts and information about a real person.

Incorrect. This is a description of a biography. In this selection, the characters and events are fictional.

TRY IT! Review the definition of realistic fiction in the **Strategies and Tips** box above. Then describe two characteristics of "The Fortune Cookie" that show it is a work of *realistic* fiction.

1. _____

_____

2. _____

_____

INSTRUCTION

Go on

Question 3   This question is about **drawing conclusions.** *Drawing conclusions* means making judgments based only on the *facts* that are presented in the selection.

Strategies and Tips for Drawing Conclusions

- A conclusion is never a wild guess. A **conclusion** is a decision or opinion that you make based on the *facts* that you have read.
- Make sure that the facts in the selection support your conclusion. For example: *In winter, the leaves fall off the trees. The trees in my backyard have no leaves* (facts). You can logically conclude from the *facts* that the season must be winter.

3   **You can draw the conclusion that Min**

   Ⓐ   is unhappy that she spent her birthday at the restaurant.

     Incorrect. There are no facts in the story to support this conclusion. In fact, the celebration is a family tradition.

   Ⓑ   will spend every Saturday with Mrs. Spencer.

     Incorrect. The facts in the story do not support the conclusion that Min will now spend every Saturday with Mrs. Spencer.

   Ⓒ   annoyed Mrs. Spencer by staying with her all day.

     Incorrect. Again, there are no facts to support this conclusion. Mrs. Spencer has a look of relief when Min decides to stay with her.

   Ⓓ   was not disappointed that she had missed the picnic.

     Correct. The facts suggest that, by the end of the day, Min was glad that she gave her time to help Mrs. Spencer, even though it meant missing the picnic.

TRY IT!   List two facts from the story that support this conclusion: *Min was kind and generous.* Skim the story for the facts.

1. _____

_____

_____

2. _____

_____

_____

_____

©2002 Options Publishing, Inc.

Question 4   This question is about **making inferences**. *Inferences* are logical guesses based on the evidence and details in the selection.

Strategies and Tips for Making Inferences

- When you do not have enough *facts* to lead you to a conclusion, you make an **inference**—a logical guess—from the details and information you are given. Writers often expect readers to make inferences. Authors do not always tell you what every character is feeling or why something has happened. You must infer what the writer has not directly stated by carefully examining the clues and details in a selection. When you make an inference, use the details from the story along with your knowledge and common sense about life.
- Read this sentence: *The eastern sky was pink and golden yellow.* The author is not telling you what time of day it is. You must infer the time of day by using your knowledge. You know that the sun rises in the east—so it must be morning.

4 **You can infer that Min stayed with Mrs. Spencer because**

(F) Min could tell that Mrs. Spencer really needed help and companionship.

Correct. All the details that Min notices—Mrs. Spencer's drapes are closed; she is in bed; her glasses are broken; she cannot make herself breakfast—suggest that Mrs. Spencer cannot get out of bed and needs help.

(G) Min's mother wanted her to stay.

Incorrect. The details in the story do not support this inference. Mrs. Li only asks Min to deliver the groceries.

(H) Min did not want to spend the entire day with friends.

Incorrect. Again, look at the details in the story. This inference is not supported by the details or information in the story.

(J) Min felt guilty about leaving Mrs. Spencer because she was ill.

Incorrect. Look at the details in paragraph 11. Min stays on an impulse, or whim, and not because she feels guilty.

TRY IT! From the details in the story, you can make an inference about Min's character. On the lines below, write a word that you think describes Min. Then list the details you used from the story to support your word choice.

_____

_____

_____

_____

_____

INSTRUCTION

©2002 Options Publishing, Inc.

Question 5
This question is about **identifying details** from the selection. **Details** are the *who, what, when, where, why,* and *how* of what you have read. This type of question checks your basic understanding of the selection.

Strategies and Tips for Identifying Details

- **Details** in a selection help you organize the information that an author gives you. They also help you keep events in order. Details are different from supporting details. Supporting details help develop the main idea. **Details** are the basics—they tell you the **5 Ws and H**: the *who, what, when, where, why,* and *how* of a story. Follow these steps to help you remember details:
- After you read the directions and introductory sentence to the selection, take a moment to **predict** what you might learn from the article. When you finish reading the selection, **reflect** on what you have read. **Reread** any parts of the selection that are still unclear.
- Do not reread the entire story to look for details. Always skim the story to find the detail asked in the question.

5 Mrs. Spencer cannot go to the store because

 Ⓐ she hurt her back.   **Correct. Skim the story. This detail is in paragraph 7.**

 Ⓑ she does not drive.   **Incorrect.** Skim the story. This detail is not in the story.

 Ⓒ her reading glasses are broken. **Incorrect.** Skim the story for the words *reading glasses.* In that paragraph, you will see that Mrs. Spencer broke her reading glasses when she fell. This is not *why* she cannot go to the store.

 Ⓓ she is expecting a visit from Min. **Incorrect.** Skim the story. Mrs. Spencer does not know that Min will visit.

TRY IT! Skim the story to find the details that answer the questions below. Write the details on the lines.

1. Who is the story mostly about?

_____

_____

2. Why does Min go to Mrs. Spencer's home?

_____

_____

©2002 Options Publishing, Inc.

No copying permitted.

Question 6   This question is about **identifying generalizations**. A *generalization* is a broad statement intended to be true about a group of people, situations, or objects.

Strategies and Tips for Identifying Generalizations

Generalizations *should* be based on facts, but some generalizations are faulty and not based on facts.

- Generalizations are often signaled by clue words: *always, never, all, most,* or *many.* When you read a generalization, evaluate it to see if it is supported by facts, and rely on your own knowledge and experiences.
- A **valid generalization** is *Some dog owners dislike cats.* The key word is *some.* There are some dog owners who dislike cats. If the generalization is supported by facts, it is true, or valid.
- Writers sometimes make errors in reasoning when they try to prove a point. A **faulty generalization** is *All dog owners dislike cats.* If even one owner likes cats, the generalization is faulty. A faulty generalization is untrue because it does not apply to *all* cases.

6   **Which of the following statements is a *valid* generalization?**

(F) Everyone in Mrs. Spencer's neighborhood liked her.

Incorrect. This is a faulty generalization. There are no facts to support the idea that *everyone* liked Mrs. Spencer.

(G) All people love to celebrate birthdays.

Incorrect. You cannot know if *all people* love to celebrate birthdays, but your knowledge of people tells you that this statement is not true.

(H) Fortune cookies often contain thought-provoking sayings.

Correct. This is valid. Fortune cookies *often* do contain sayings that make you think about life in general.

(J) Everyone can help the elderly at the senior center.

Incorrect. Not *all* people may be physically or mentally capable of helping.

TRY IT!   At the end of each statement, write **Faulty** for a faulty generalization and **Valid** for a valid generalization. Then explain *why* each statement is valid or faulty.

1. Many people feel helpless without their eyeglasses. _____

_____

_____

2. Summer days are always sunny. _____

_____

_____

INSTRUCTION

©2002 Options Publishing, Inc.

Go on

Question 7   This question is about **identifying fact and opinion**. A *fact* can be proved. An *opinion* cannot be proved or disproved. An opinion is based on what someone thinks, feels, or believes.

Strategies and Tips for Identifying Fact and Opinion

- A **fact** is a statement that can be proved. It is supposed to be true or to have really happened. *Min does not have school on Saturday* is a fact. Look at paragraph 4. The author tells you that it is Saturday, and Min says, "No school."
- An **opinion** is a statement about what someone feels or thinks. It cannot be proved or disproved. *Min loves Saturdays* is an opinion. The word *loves* signals a feeling—and feelings are opinions. Words that describe how a person feels or thinks always signal an opinion: *sad, happy, angry, pleased, love, hate, beautiful,* or *wonderful.* An opinion tells what someone feels or believes.

7   **Which of the following statements is an opinion?**

Ⓐ Carol called to say that they couldn't wait any longer for Min.

Incorrect. This is a fact that can be proved. Mrs. Li gave Min this message.

Ⓑ Mrs. Spencer hurt her back.

Incorrect. This is a fact. The story tells you that Mrs. Spencer cannot get out to the stores because she hurt her back.

Ⓒ Min was pleased with herself for helping Mrs. Spencer.

Correct. This is an opinion. The word *pleased* describes a feeling, and feelings are opinions.

Ⓓ Min and her friends had planned a picnic in the park.

Incorrect. This is also a fact. Look in paragraph 4. The author tells you they made these plans.

TRY IT! How well do you understand fact and opinion? On the lines below, rewrite each fact statement as an opinion. The first one is done for you.

1. It is a Li family tradition to celebrate birthdays at the Chinese restaurant.

The Li family loves to celebrate birthdays at the Chinese restaurant. (Notice that the word *loves* is added to make the statement an opinion.)

2. Min fixed breakfast for Mrs. Spencer.

_____

3. On Saturday morning, Min did a favor for her mother.

_____

©2002 Options Publishing, Inc.

No copying permitted.

Question 8   This question is about understanding a word by **using context clues**. *Context clues* are found in the words and sentences before or after the unfamiliar word. They give clues, or hints, to the meaning of the unfamiliar word.

Strategies and Tips for Using Context Clues

Context clues refer to the words or sentences before or after an unfamiliar word. When you read, authors often use words that are unfamiliar to you. You can frequently determine what that word means by seeing how it is used in the sentence or in the paragraph. Sometimes, authors give you very specific clues:

- **Synonym clue:** A **synonym** is a word that means the same or nearly the same as the unfamiliar word. *On an impulse, or whim, Min asked if she could get the mail for Mrs. Spencer.* The author provides the synonym *whim* to help you understand the word *impulse.*
- **Definition clue:** The author gives you the **definition** of the unfamiliar word. *At the Chinese restaurant, we ordered chau tse—a Chinese dumpling filled with meat and vegetables and cooked in boiling water.*
- **Example clue:** The author gives you an **example** of the unfamiliar word. *I received a beautiful bouquet of flowers. It was carefully tied together and wrapped in green florist paper.*

8 "Mrs. Spencer looked *frailer* and more fragile than Min remembered her."
The word *frailer* means

Ⓕ stronger.   **Incorrect.** This word means the opposite of the words *frail* and *fragile*

Ⓖ healthier.   **Incorrect.** This does not make sense with the word *fragile*. How can someone be *healthier* and *more fragile*?

Ⓗ weaker.   **Correct. The author gives you a clue by adding the words *more fragile*. If someone is frail and fragile, you know that he or she must be weak.**

Ⓙ tougher.   **Incorrect.** This also does not make sense. Can a person be *tough* and *fragile*?

TRY IT! Read the sentences below. Circle the word or group of words that gives clues to the meaning of the word in boldface.

1. "Min, are you awake?" Her mother's voice **roused** her from her daydreams.

2. She could see from the look of **relief** on Mrs. Spencer's face that this was a very welcome offer.

INSTRUCTION

Go on

©2002 Options Publishing, Inc.

No copying permitted.   Comprehensive Reading and Writing Assessment 8   77

Directions

Here is the article "A Computer to Talk To" that appeared in Test A. Reread the article, and then compare your answers with the answers given here. Read *Strategies and Tips* to learn how to find the correct answer, and use the *TRY IT!* activities for additional practice.

A Computer to Talk To

Richard knew the Karachi airport and the airspace around it well, having taken off from here several times before. His checklist complete, he adjusted his headset, glanced at the cockpit dials, and looked down the runway.

"Tower, Cessna 916, Runway 14," he said. "Request takeoff clearance."

"Cleared for takeoff," came the reply in his earpiece. The voice was female. The accent was Pakistani. Richard opened the throttle.

Then his mother came into the room. "I know you love that computer game, but it's time to stop playing and start your homework."

The game Richard was playing is a flight simulator game that allows the player to experience what it is like to fly. It has two software improvements: One improvement stores and plays 25,000 prerecorded audio clips—the stock phrases that air traffic controllers use to communicate with pilots. These clips, or phrases, are spoken in the accented English of controllers in forty different parts of the world. The second improvement is *voice recognition software*. This software translates human speech—the words Richard used—into signals that a computer can understand. The result is that the game gives Richard a true-to-life flight experience. He gets the feeling he is really controlling the plane because the pilot and air traffic controller have conversations that are a natural part of flying.

One goal of the engineers who develop computer systems is to have computers adapt to people rather than have people adapt to computers. This means getting computers to communicate, or talk, in ways that are natural. Computer developers want people to be able to talk to their computers instead of using devices. The keyboard and mouse could be replaced by a person's voice!

©2002 Options Publishing, Inc.

Speech is natural for human beings. We learn to speak at an early age. Most computers can play music and produce sound effects. Many can also speak words and talk to us. However, getting computers to understand what *we* say to them is very difficult. Why?

Well, to understand speech, a computer must recognize *all* the individual sounds that make up each word. For example, the spoken word *cat* has three sounds. It has a *k* sound at the beginning, a short *a* sound in the middle, and a *t* sound at the end. Think of words that begin with the letter *c* and the different sounds within each word: *cat, cool, chin,* or *ceiling.* And to make matters more difficult, people in different parts of the country or the world speak English with different accents. English also sounds different when spoken in a continuous speech pattern rather than pronouncing each word—One—Word—At—A—Time.

For a computer to sort out all these sounds requires a huge amount of processing power. Only recently has this power been available at affordable prices. So it's no surprise that one of the first games to use voice recognition software can understand only a few sets of phrases—in this case, the phrases that pilots use when they talk to control towers. If you tried to read a poem or a grocery list to the flight simulator game, it wouldn't know what to do!

Systems that understand enough words so that you can talk to them are still very expensive. They require a much more powerful computer than most of us have on our desks. When those systems do become available at affordable prices, some people may still prefer to use the traditional keyboard and mouse. However, many people may like the freedom of using their voice rather than their fingertips on a keyboard. Imagine, you might "speak" your next book report into your computer, and the computer will put your words onto the page! Voice recognition systems will give independence to physically challenged people who cannot type or see the screen or keyboard.

And, for those of us who love computer games, there are some really cool voice-operated games coming!

©2002 Options Publishing, Inc.

INSTRUCTION

Go on

Question 9   This question is about **identifying the main idea** of a selection. The *main idea* is the topic of a selection. It is the most important idea or thought that the author wants the reader to understand.

Strategies and Tips for Identifying the Main Idea

A **main idea** statement answers two questions:

- It tells you *who* or *what* the subject, or topic, of the selection is about. In "A Computer to Talk To," the main idea answers the question: *What is the subject, or topic?* The subject in this article is about voice recognition software.

- It answers the question *does what?* or *is what?* or *how?* about the topic. In this article, the main idea statement answers *does what*. The main idea explains *what* voice recognition *does*.

- When you make a main idea statement, be sure that it is not *too broad* or *too narrow*. If you said this article was about computer software, your statement would be *too broad*. It is too general and does not tell enough about the topic. If you said that the article was about a flight simulation game, the statement would be *too narrow*. The game is a detail in the article and used as an example.

9 **This article is mostly about**

Ⓐ   computer games.

Incorrect. This statement is *too broad* and *too general*. It does not tell you what the topic is about. Be sure to read *all* the answer choices.

Ⓑ   voice recognition software and what it does.

Correct. This describes the *main idea*. It tells you *what* the topic of the article is about (voice recognition). It also tells *what* this software does.

Ⓒ   voice recognition will be useful for physically challenged people.

Incorrect. This statement is *too narrow*. It is a detail from the article.

Ⓓ   how people speak English with different accents.

Incorrect. This statement is *too narrow*. It is one detail from the article.

TRY IT! The title of this article is "A Computer to Talk To." Using the main idea of this article, briefly explain on the lines below why you think the author chose this title.

_____

_____

_____

_____

©2002 Options Publishing, Inc.

No copying permitted.

Question 10   This question is about **identifying supporting details**. *Supporting details* support, or build on, the main idea. They further explain, clarify, or examine the main idea.

Strategies and Tips for Identifying Supporting Details

Supporting details support, or build on, the main idea. To identify supporting details:

- Think about the **main idea**, or main point, of the article. In "A Computer to Talk To," the main idea is about voice recognition software and what it does. The details within the article must support this main idea.

- Without **supporting details**, a main idea can be difficult to accept or understand. If the author had not given you the example of voice recognition software used in a game, you might have a difficult time understanding just what this software does. By giving the example, the author supports his main idea and presents you with an article that makes sense and is easy to understand

10 **Which detail from the article *best* supports the main idea of the article?**

(F) Voice recognition software translates human speech into signals that a computer can understand.

Correct. This detail best supports the main idea. It explains what voice recognition software does.

(G) The word *cat* is made up of three different sounds.

Incorrect. This is not the best support for the main idea. It is a small detail in the article.

(H) Most computers can play music and produce sound effects.

Incorrect. This is a small detail. It is not the best support for the main idea.

(J) The air traffic controller spoke with a Pakistani accent.

Incorrect. This is a minor detail from the article and does not support the main idea.

TRY IT!   Reread paragraph 6 in the article. On the lines below, write the main idea sentence (topic sentence) from the paragraph. Then write one detail from the paragraph that supports the main idea.

Main Idea: _____

_____

_____

Supporting Details: _____

_____

_____

INSTRUCTION

Go on

©2002 Options Publishing, Inc.

No copying permitted.   Comprehensive Reading and Writing Assessment 8   81

Question 11   This question is about **identifying cause-and-effect** relationships. A *cause* is an action that brings about a result, or *effect*.

Strategies and Tips for Identifying Cause and Effect

Sometimes, one event causes another event to happen. Authors use cause and effect to help you understand *why* something happens.

- One way to recognize a cause-and-effect statement is to look for words that *signal* the relationship: *because, therefore, since, before, after, as a result.* For example: *The earth turns* (cause); *therefore, the sun appears to rise and set* (effect).

- Sometimes, the order is reversed and the effect comes before the cause: *The sun appears to rise and set* (effect) *because the earth turns* (cause).

11   **Getting computers to understand what we say is difficult because**

Ⓐ computers can only speak words.

Incorrect. This is not a logical cause, or reason, for *why* it is difficult for computers to understand spoken language.

Ⓑ computer equipment is very expensive.

Incorrect. Ask yourself: Is this a logical reason for *why* computers have difficulty understanding spoken language? It does not explain why.

Ⓒ people do not want computers with voice recognition software.

Incorrect. Again, this does not explain *why* computers cannot understand spoken language.

Ⓓ computers must recognize the separate sounds within every word.

Correct. Because computers must recognize the separate sounds within every word (cause), getting computers to understand what we say is difficult (effect).

TRY IT!   Reread the **Strategies and Tips** above. Then draws lines to match the cause with the correct effect. The first one is done for you.

Cause	Effect
1. Because computers with voice recognition require a huge amount of processing power,	as a result, those people who cannot type or see the screen or keyboard will be able to use a computer.
2. With voice recognition software, people can speak directly to the computer;	the game understands basic phrases used by air traffic controllers.
3. Since the flight simulator game has voice recognition software,	these computers were very expensive in the past.

©2002 Options Publishing, Inc.

No copying permitted.

Question 12   This question is about **drawing conclusions**. *Drawing conclusions* means making judgments based only on the *facts* that are presented in the selection.

Strategies and Tips for Drawing Conclusions

- A conclusion is never a wild guess. A **conclusion** is a decision or opinion that you make based on the *facts* that you have read.
- Make sure that the facts in the selection support your conclusion. For example, you can conclude from the facts in the article that as computers increase their processing power, voice recognition software will continue to improve. Reread paragraphs 8 and 9. You will find the facts that support this conclusion.

12   **From the facts in the article, you can conclude that voice recognition software**

Ⓕ will always need computers that are too expensive.

Incorrect. The facts in the article do not support this conclusion. In fact, the cost of the computers needed to run the software is coming down.

Ⓖ will become more popular as powerful computers become less expensive.

Correct. This is a logical conclusion from the *facts* given. The powerful computers are becoming less expensive.

Ⓗ will be used only in computer games.

Incorrect. The article gives facts that support just the opposite conclusion. Voice recognition software will be used for more than computer games.

Ⓙ will never be popular because it is too difficult to use.

Incorrect. Look at the facts in the article. They suggest that this software is improving all the time.

TRY IT! The author concludes that "voice recognition software will give independence to physically challenged people who cannot type or see the screen or keyboard." On the lines below, write one fact from the article that supports this conclusion.

_____

_____

_____

INSTRUCTION

©2002 Options Publishing, Inc.

Go on

Question 13   This question is about **making inferences**. *Inferences* are logical guesses based on the evidence and details in the selection.

Strategies and Tips for Making Inferences

- When you do not have enough *facts* to lead you to a conclusion, you make an **inference**—a logical guess—from the information you are given. Writers often expect readers to make inferences; that is, some questions cannot be answered by the facts alone. You must "read between the lines." Use details from the selection along with your knowledge and common sense to infer what the writer has not directly stated. Always carefully examine clues or hints.
- Read this sentence: *Marie stood on the sidewalk. The tall buildings surrounding her blocked her view of the sky.* You can logically infer that Maria is in a city. However, you must not assume too much. You *cannot* infer that Marie lives in the city. The details do not support that inference. Maria may be visiting the city. Always go back to the selection to check the details.

13 **From the details in the article, you can infer that Richard is taking off from an airport in**

Ⓐ England.

Incorrect. There are no details in the article to support this inference.

Ⓑ the United States.

Incorrect. Again, there are no details in the article to support this inference.

Ⓒ Pakistan.

Correct. Look at the details in paragraphs 1 and 3. Even if you do not know where Karachi is, the author tells you the air traffic controller has a Pakistani accent. It is logical to infer that Karachi is in Pakistan.

Ⓓ Russia.

Incorrect. Look at the first few paragraphs. There are no details that suggest the airfield is in Russia.

TRY IT! Authors often expect you to make inferences from the details they give you. Read the following descriptions. Use the details to infer the time of day or the time of year. Write your answer on the lines.

1. The drifting snow made it impossible for cars and buses to pass along the streets.

Time of year: _____

2. As Maria gazed into the sky, she was able to make out the Big and Little Dippers.

Time of day: _____

3. As they stepped out into the brisk morning, they were surprised by the red and gold leaves fluttering down to the ground.

Time of year: _____

©2002 Options Publishing, Inc.

No copying permitted.

Question 14
This question is about **identifying details** from the selection. *Details* are the *who, what, when, where, why,* and *how* of what you have read. This type of question checks your basic understanding of the selection.

Strategies and Tips for Identifying Details

- **Details** in a selection help you organize the information that an author gives you. They also help you keep events in order. Details are different from supporting details. Supporting details help develop the main idea. **Details** are the basics—they tell you the **5 Ws and H**: the *who, what, when, where, why,* and *how* of a story. Follow these steps to help you remember details:
- After you read the directions and introductory sentence to the selection, take a moment to **predict** what you might learn from the article. When you finish reading the selection, **reflect** on what you have read. **Reread** any parts of the selection that were unclear.
- Do not reread the entire story to look for details. Always skim the story to find the detail asked in the question.

14 **What was one of the software improvements to Richard's flight simulator game?**

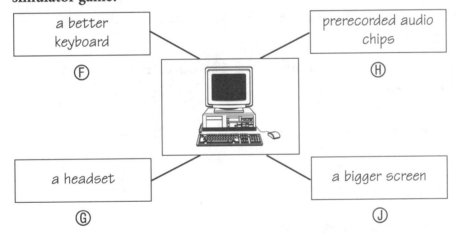

| a better keyboard (F) | prerecorded audio chips (H) |
| a headset (G) | a bigger screen (J) |

Answer H, *prerecorded audio chips,* **is correct.**

Answers F, G, and H are not software improvements. Skim paragraph 5 in the article to find the correct answer.

TRY IT! Write two details, or facts, that you learned from the article about voice recognition software.

1. _____

_____

2. _____

_____

INSTRUCTION

Go on

©2002 Options Publishing, Inc.

No copying permitted.

Question 15   This question is about **identifying sequence**. *Sequence* is the particular order of a series of events or ideas.

Strategies and Tips for Identifying Sequence

- **Chronological order**, or time sequence, is the order in which events occur. Sometimes, the order of events is clear: One event simply follows the other. At other times, the author may use words that signal chronological order: *first, last, then, next, often.*
- Sequence is a kind of organization that helps you make sense of the events.
- Before you mark your final answer, be sure to read *all* the answer choices.

15 **Which of the following details occurs *first* in the article?**

Ⓐ an explanation of what voice recognition software does

Correct. Skim the article for the words *voice recognition*. This detail occurs first in the article—in paragraph 5.

Ⓑ an explanation of how words are made up of individual sounds

Incorrect. This detail comes later in the article.

Ⓒ some people may prefer to use the traditional keyboard and mouse

Incorrect. This detail comes last in the article.

Ⓓ the flight simulator game can understand only a few sets of phrases

Incorrect. This detail comes later in the article.

TRY IT! Put the following details in the order in which they occurred in the article. Skim the story for the details.

_____ The spoken word *cat* has three sounds.

_____ The flight simulator game has two software improvements.

_____ Richard knows the Karachi airport very well.

_____ The flight simulator game can understand only a few sets of phrases.

©2002 Options Publishing, Inc.

No copying permitted.

Question 16   This question is about **identifying fact and opinion**. A *fact* can be proved. An *opinion* cannot be proved or disproved. An opinion is based on what someone thinks, feels, or believes.

Strategies and Tips for Identifying Fact and Opinion

- A **fact** is a statement that can be proved. It is supposed to be true or to have really happened. *People in different parts of the country or the world speak English with different accents* is a fact. This statement can be proved.

- An **opinion** is a statement about what someone feels or thinks. It cannot be proved or disproved. For example, Richard's mother states an opinion: *"I know you love that computer game . . ."* The word *love* signals a feeling—and feelings are opinions. Words that describe how a person feels always signal an opinion: *sad, happy, angry, pleased, love, hate, beautiful,* or *wonderful.* An opinion tells what someone feels or believes.

16 **Which of the following statements is an opinion?**

(F) Speech is natural for human beings. We learn to speak at an early age.

Incorrect. This is fact that can be proved by reading information about humans and speech.

(G) Every word is made up of individual sounds.

Incorrect. Your knowledge of words tells you that this is a fact.

(H) Games that use voice recognition software are more fun to play.

Correct. This is an opinion. The phrase "more fun to play" describes a feeling, and feelings are opinions.

(J) Computers that understand spoken words require a huge amount of processing power.

Incorrect. This is also a fact. You can prove it by researching information about voice recognition systems.

TRY IT! Reread paragraph 10 in the article. On the lines below, write one opinion and one fact that you find in that paragraph.

Fact: _____

_____

_____

Opinion: _____

_____

_____

INSTRUCTION

©2002 Options Publishing, Inc.

Go on

Question 17 This question is about **identifying the genre** of a selection. The *genre* identifies the type of literary work, such as nonfiction, fiction, poetry, and drama. Each genre has its own unique characteristics.

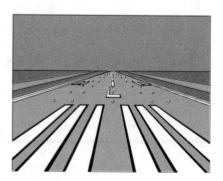

Strategies and Tips for Identifying Genre

Literary genre refers to the type of literature you read.

- **Fiction** is writing that uses characters and events that are not real. Myths, folktales, and many short stories are fiction.
- **Nonfiction** is writing that uses real people, places, and events. Articles, essays, biographies, autobiographies, and profiles are all nonfiction. They are about real people, places, or events.
- "A Computer to Talk To" is an article. **Articles** inform or explain a subject to readers and are generally found in newspapers and magazines. Articles are usually objective; that is, they present facts rather than feelings or opinions.

17 "A Computer to Talk To" can best be described as

Ⓐ a fictional short story.

Incorrect. A fictional short story is about characters and events that are not real.

Ⓑ a biography.

Incorrect. A biography gives information about a real person.

Ⓒ a play.

Incorrect. A play is drama and has a cast of characters.

Ⓓ an article.

Correct. This selection is an article because it gives information and presents facts rather than feelings or opinions.

TRY IT! On the lines below, explain what characteristics make "A Computer to Talk To" a work of nonfiction.

_____

_____

_____

_____

©2002 Options Publishing, Inc.

Question 18   This question is about understanding a word by **using context clues**. *Context clues* are found in the words and sentences before or after the unfamiliar word. They give clues, or hints, to the meaning of the unfamiliar word.

Strategies and Tips for Using Context Clues

Context clues refer to the words or sentences before or after an unfamiliar word.

- When you read, you are often faced with a word that you do not know. You can frequently determine what that word means by seeing how it is used in the sentence or in the paragraph. Sometimes, authors give you very specific clues:

- **Example clues:** The author gives you an example of the unfamiliar word. *Our football team is made up of greenhorns. Not one member has played football before!* Notice that the author gives you an example that helps you understand the meaning of *greenhorn*.

- Before you mark the answer you think is correct, be sure to read *all* the choices.

18   "Computer developers want people to be able to talk to their computers instead of using *devices*. The keyboard and mouse could be replaced by a person's voice!"
The word *devices* means

Ⓕ	equipment.	**Correct. Can you find the context clues? The author adds the words *keyboard and mouse* to help you understand that devices means "equipment."**
Ⓖ	jobs.	**Incorrect.** Try reading the sentence using the word *jobs* in place of *devices*. It does not make sense.
Ⓗ	computers.	**Incorrect.** Again, this word does not make sense when it is used in the sentence.
Ⓙ	plans.	**Incorrect.** You must read the sentence carefully. Then try using the word in the sentence. The word *plans* does not make sense..

TRY IT! Review the information about example clues in the **Strategies and Tips** box above. Go back to the article and skim for the words *voice recognition*. Then read the sentence below. Rewrite the sentence by adding an example that gives a clue to the meaning of the expression in boldface.

My computer game uses **voice recognition** software.

_____

_____

_____

©2002 Options Publishing, Inc.

INSTRUCTION

Go on

Directions

Here is the historical fiction journal "The Journal of Emma Scars" that appeared in Test A. Reread the story, and then compare *your* answers with the answers given here. Read *Strategies and Tips* to learn how to find the correct answer, and use the *TRY IT!* activities for additional practice.

The Journal of Emma Scars

In the 1800s, sailing ships transported most raw materials and manufactured goods around the world. Whaling boats and tall-masted clipper ships crisscrossed the oceans, sometimes on journeys lasting as long as two years. Often, the wives of the ships' captains traveled with their husbands. Many of these women kept journals or sent letters home describing their adventures at sea.

This journal is called historical fiction. The author took real events from the past and built a fictional character and journal around the events.

◆

May 10, 1849, South Pacific

I write from our cabin somewhere in the South Seas. I am so proud of Edward as he issues orders to trim the sails and bring the ship about. Our ship is quite glorious under sail. I spend my days writing letters, reading novels, doing Edward's laundry, and supervising the cook. The weather has been lovely and we are making good progress. Most of the seamen are caring and hardworking, although rather rough sorts. They call our ship a "hen frigate," meaning that there is a woman on board. They are not pleased to have me aboard, as they think this will bring bad luck. However, I am determined to change their minds by befriending them, while keeping out of their way.

The clipper ship *Flying Cloud* sailed in 1851. It is typical of the type of ship Emma and her husband sailed.

Why do you suppose that young women are not permitted to attend maritime academies to learn to navigate and command grand ships, such as Edward's? Such skills seem far more stimulating than darning socks and stitching samplers!

June 19, 1849, South Pacific

We have spent three days sitting in the Doldrums, which is a hot, airless

©2002 Options Publishing, Inc.

No copying permitted.

calm. Since we have no wind or even a breeze, we cannot make any progress. Edward wears a fierce scowl, worrying constantly about the time we must make up to deliver our cargo.

The crew is bored and restless. To relieve the tedium, the men caught a shark and brought it on board, which entertained us for a few hours and raised the spirits of those on the ship. I still beg Edward to teach me navigation skills, and he has agreed, somewhat reluctantly. He does not think a woman needs to know these things, but he will teach me anyway. We take "sightings" of the stars on clear nights. To navigate, or set a course, for the ship, I must learn a great deal of mathematics and trigonometry, which I truly enjoy.

August 23, 1849, South Pacific

Two nights ago, I stayed up many hours nursing Edward, who is ill with a fever. I was bathing his forehead with a towel soaked in seawater when the first mate came in to announce the sighting of storm clouds. Without Edward to navigate, the men worry about becoming caught in the storm and losing our direction.

Typical clothing worn by a Victorian woman.

I entered the captain's bridge and began my calculations to help us navigate clear of the storm. I gave orders to adjust the sails to catch the breeze and then set our course. I was determined that we should make haste to leave this deadly calm and outrun the storm that chased us. To my amazement, none of the men refused or balked at my command! It was my good fortune to earn their trust and friendship early in the voyage.

Unfortunately, we could not outrun the storm. The main mast snapped with a fierce crack as thunder rolled and lightning struck all around us that night. The men pulled together under my command to shorten the canvas sails and steer us from the crest of one huge wave to the next. I tied myself onto the bridge so that the waves could not sweep me overboard. I have never been so frightened in my life, yet I did not let the men see, for I knew they would no longer heed my orders if they sensed any weakness.

It was exhilarating to be in command and using my brain! It seems clear to me now that all young women must have an education and an opportunity to exercise their mental powers through challenging labor. I am determined to raise my daughters to do so, and am resolved to spread this idea of education upon my return home.

©2002 Options Publishing, Inc.

Go on

INSTRUCTION

Question 19

This question is about **identifying the main idea** of a selection. The *main idea* is the topic of a selection. It is the most important idea or thought that the author wants the reader to understand.

Strategies and Tips for Identifying the Main Idea

A **main idea** statement answers two questions:

- It tells you *who* or *what* the subject, or topic, of the selection is about. In "The Journal of Emma Scars," the main idea answers the question: *Who* is this journal about? It is about Emma Scars, the wife of a ship's captain.

- It answers the question *does what?* or *is what?* or *how?* about the topic. In this journal, the main idea statement answers *does what.* The main idea explains *what* Emma experiences and how she learned to navigate the ship.

- When you make a main idea statement, be sure that it is not *too broad* or *too narrow.* If you said this journal was about sailing ships, your statement is *too broad.* It is too general and does not tell enough about the topic. If you said that the article was about the main mast breaking during a storm, the statement is *too narrow.* This event is one small detail in the article.

19 **This selection is mostly about**

Ⓐ delivering cargo by ship during the 1800s.

Incorrect. This statement is *too broad* and *too general.* It does not tell you what the topic is about. Be sure to read *all* the answer choices.

Ⓑ a severe storm at sea during the 1800s.

Incorrect. This statement is *too narrow.* It is a detail from the selection.

Ⓒ sailing conditions during the 1800s.

Incorrect. This statement is *too broad.* It does not give you much information about who the selection is about or what the person does.

Ⓓ a woman learns to navigate a ship during the 1800s.

Correct. This describes the *main idea.* It tells you *who* the journal is about (Emma Scars). It also tells *what* she does—navigates the ship.

TRY IT! Skim the journal. Then, in your own words, write a brief summary of the selection. Be sure to include *who* the selection is about and *what* that person does or accomplishes.

_____

_____

_____

_____

No copying permitted.

©2002 Options Publishing, Inc.

Question 20   This question is about **identifying supporting details**. *Supporting details* support, or build on, the main idea. They further explain, clarify, or examine the main idea.

Strategies and Tips for Identifying Supporting Details

Supporting details support, or build on, the main idea. To identify supporting details:

- Think about the **main idea**, or main point, of the selection. In "The Journal of Emma Scars," the main idea is about a woman, Emma Scars, and what she does. The details within the journal must support this main idea.

- Without **supporting details**, a main idea can be difficult to accept or understand. If the author had not given you an example of Emma using her navigation skills during and after the storm, you might have a difficult time understanding just what Emma accomplishes on her journey. By giving the example, the author supports the main idea and presents you with a journal that makes sense and is easy to understand.

20 **Which detail *best* supports the main idea of the journal?**

Ⓕ The crew is bored and restless.

Incorrect. This is not the best support for the main idea. It is a small detail in the journal.

Ⓖ Two nights ago, I stayed up many hours nursing Edward, who is ill with a fever.

Incorrect. This is a small detail. It is not the best support for the main idea.

Ⓗ To navigate, or set a course, for the ship, I must learn a great deal of mathematics and trigonometry, which I truly enjoy.

Correct. This detail best supports the main idea. It explains what Emma learns and accomplishes on the sailing journey.

Ⓙ The main mast snapped with a fierce crack as thunder rolled and lightning struck all around us that night.

Incorrect. This is a small detail from the journal and does not support the main idea.

TRY IT! How do you think Emma feels about women receiving an education? Write your answer on the lines below. Then list two details from the journal that support your answer.

_____

_____

Supporting Detail: _____

_____

Supporting Detail: _____

_____

©2002 Options Publishing, Inc.

No copying permitted.

Go on

INSTRUCTION

Question 21   This question is about **identifying sequence.** *Sequence* is the particular order of a series of events or ideas.

Strategies and Tips for Identifying Sequence

- **Chronological order,** or time sequence, is the order in which events occur. Sometimes, the order of events is clear: One event simply follows the other. At other times, the author may use words that signal chronological order: *first, last, then, next, often.*
- Sequence is a kind of organization that helps you make sense of the events.
- Before you mark your final answer, be sure to read *all* the answer choices.

21 **Which of the following details occurs *last* in the journal?**

Ⓐ Emma commands the ship through a storm.

Correct. Skim the article for the word *storm*. This detail occurs last in the journal—in the August 23, 1849, entry.

Ⓑ Emma befriends the crew.

Incorrect. This detail occurs first in the journal.

Ⓒ Emma learns to navigate.

Incorrect. This detail occurs second in the journal.

Ⓓ Emma nurses Edward, who has a fever.

Incorrect. This is the third detail in the journal.

TRY IT! Put the following details in the order in which they occurred in the journal. Skim the journal for the details.

_____ Emma is determined to see that her daughters receive an education.

_____ Emma ties herself to the bridge.

_____ The crew brings a shark on board.

_____ The ship is stuck in the Doldrums—a hot, airless calm.

Clippership *Comet* of New York.

No copying permitted.

©2002 Options Publishing, Inc.

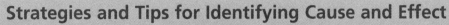

Question 22   This question is about **identifying cause-and-effect** relationships. A *cause* is an action that brings about a result, or *effect*.

Strategies and Tips for Identifying Cause and Effect

Sometimes, one event causes another event to happen. Authors use cause and effect to help you understand *why* something happens.

- One way to recognize a cause-and-effect statement is to look for words that *signal* the relationship: *because, therefore, since, before, after, as a result*. For example: *The earth turns* (cause); *therefore, the sun appears to rise and set* (effect).
- Sometimes, the order is reversed and the effect comes before the cause: *The sun appears to rise and set* (effect) *because the earth turns* (cause).

22 **The storm is so violent that Emma worries that waves will wash her overboard; as a result,**

   Ⓕ she ties herself to the bridge.

         Correct. Because the waves could wash Emma overboard (cause), she ties herself to the bridge (effect).

   Ⓖ she goes to her cabin.

         Incorrect. This effect, or result, is not mentioned in the journal.

   Ⓗ she navigates the ship out of the storm.

         Incorrect. This does not explain *why* Emma worries about the waves.

   Ⓙ she has the crew shorten the canvas sails.

         Incorrect. Again, this does not explain *why* Emma worries about the waves. She has the crew shorten the sails because the main mast breaks.

TRY IT! Reread the **Strategies and Tips** above. Then complete the chart by writing in the correct cause or effect to complete each statement. Be sure to skim the journal for the correct cause or effect.

Cause	Effect
1. Because the crew thinks a woman on board brings bad luck,	_____ _____ _____
2. _____ _____ _____	Edward is reluctant to teach Emma navigation skills.

Go on

©2002 Options Publishing, Inc.

INSTRUCTION

Question 23   This question is about **identifying generalizations**. A *generalization* is a broad statement intended to be true about a group of people, situations, or objects.

Strategies and Tips for Identifying Generalizations

Generalizations *should* be based on facts, but some generalizations are faulty and not based on facts.

- Generalizations are often signaled by clue words: *always, never, all, most,* or *many.* When you read a generalization, evaluate it to see if it is supported by facts, and rely on your own knowledge and experiences.
- A **valid generalization** is *Many people like to ride bicycles.* The key word is *many.* Many people like to ride bikes. If the generalization is supported by facts, it is true, or valid.
- Writers sometimes make errors in reasoning when they try to prove a point. A **faulty generalization** is *All people like to ride bicycles.* If even one person dislikes riding a bike, the generalization is faulty. A faulty generalization is untrue because it does not apply to *all* cases.

23 **Which of the following is a *valid* generalization?**

ⓐ Women do not possess the same mathematical skills as men.

Incorrect. This is faulty, or untrue, because it does not apply to all cases. Your knowledge and experience tells you that many women do posses mathematical skills.

ⓑ Women make better sea captains than men.

Incorrect. This is also faulty. Again, your knowledge and experience tells you that this is a broad statement, and it does not apply to all cases.

ⓒ Women in the past did not have the same opportunities that they have today.

Correct. This generalization is supported by the facts in the journal and your knowledge of history.

ⓓ Many women commanded clipper ships and whaling ships.

Incorrect. This is not a true statement.

TRY IT! You will generalize about "The Journal of Emma Scars." There are two columns below. On the left, you will find details to generalize about; on the right, you will write your generalizations. The first one is done for you.

What to Generalize About

1. The crew's attitude about women on board.

2. Edward's attitude about women learning navigation skills.

3. Emma's attitude about women's education.

Your Generalization

1. The sailors on the ship believed that a woman on board brought bad luck.

2. _____

    _____

3. _____

    _____

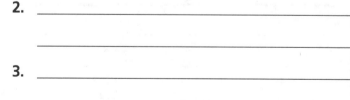

©2002 Options Publishing, Inc.

No copying permitted.

Question 24   This question is about **identifying the author's purpose** for writing. The *author's purpose* is the reason he or she wrote the selection.

Strategies and Tips for Identifying the Author's Purpose

An author usually has two purposes for writing—a **general purpose** and a **specific purpose**. Knowing an author's purpose helps you judge the writer and the selection fairly.

- The **general purpose** might be to entertain, to persuade, to inform, to explain, or to describe. "The Journal of Emma Scars" *describes* Emma's experiences and reinforces the message that women can accomplish a great deal when they are given a chance.
- The **specific purpose** is tied to the theme of the story and is the main point the author wants to make about the topic. Often, the author reinforces the specific purpose in the closing paragraph of the selection. The theme is expressed in the last paragraph of the journal: Emma realizes that women must have an education and an opportunity to exercise their mental powers.

24   **What is the author's purpose in writing this journal?**

  Ⓕ to persuade other women to stitch samplers

    Incorrect. This detail does not tie in with the theme. The author wants you to see that women can accomplish a great deal if given an education.

  Ⓖ to describe Emma's experiences and show the importance of education for women

    Correct. This is the author's purpose. The journal focuses on Emma's experiences and how she learned to navigate.

  Ⓗ to explain how to navigate a ship in the South Pacific

    Incorrect. This is not the main purpose; it is a minor detail.

  Ⓙ to entertain readers with a humorous story about life at sea

    Incorrect. The story is not amusing or humorous.

TRY IT! To help identify the author's purpose for writing, answer the following questions.

1. What specific idea does the author want to communicate to me?

_____

_____

_____

2. How does the author want me to respond after reading this journal?

_____

INSTRUCTION

©2002 Options Publishing, Inc.

No copying permitted.

Go on

Question 25   This question is about understanding a word by **using context clues**. *Context clues* are found in the words and sentences before or after the unfamiliar word. They give clues, or hints, to the meaning of the unfamiliar word.

Strategies and Tips for Using Context Clues

Context clues refer to the words or sentences before or after an unfamiliar word. When you read, authors often use words that are unfamiliar to you. You can frequently determine what that word means by seeing how it is used in the sentence or in the paragraph. Sometimes, authors give you very specific clues:

• **Synonym clue:** A synonym is a word that means the same or nearly the same as the unfamiliar word. *To my amazement, none of the men refused or <u>balked</u> at my command!* The author provides the synonym *refused* to help you understand the word *balked*.

• Remember, when you answer multiple-choice questions, be sure to read *all* the choices.

25 "The crew is bored and restless. To relieve the *tedium*, the men caught a shark and brought it on board. . . ." The word *tedium* means

(A) excitement.   **Incorrect.** Read the sentence replacing the word *tedium* with *excitement*. This word does not make sense—it is the opposite of *tedium*.

(B) boredom.   **Correct. The author gives you a clue by including the synonyms *bored* and *restless*. If you suffer from *tedium*, you are bored and restless.**

(C) eagerness.   **Incorrect.** Again, read the sentence carefully. Does it make sense that the crew is bored, restless, and eager?

(D) peacefulness.   **Incorrect.** If the crew experienced peacefulness, the sailors would not be bored or restless.

TRY IT! Sometimes authors give you a **definition clue**; that is, the author defines the unfamiliar word. Read the following sentence. Circle the definition clue for *maritime*. Then, on the lines below, describe what a maritime academy teaches.

Emma asks, "Why do you suppose that young women are not permitted to attend *maritime* academies to learn to navigate and command grand ships, such as Edward's?"

_____

_____

Stop

©2002 Options Publishing, Inc.

No copying permitted.

Directions

In this part of the test, you will either read or listen to two creation myths: "Why the Fawn Has Spots" and "Pushing Up the Sky." Then you will answer questions to demonstrate how well you understood what you read or how well you listened to what was read to you.

• If this is a Reading Session, your teacher will give you copies of the two creation myths.

• If this is a Listening Session, your teacher will read the selections to you. You will listen to the selections twice. The first time you hear the selections, listen carefully but do not take notes. When you listen to the selections the second time, you will take notes. Use your notes to answer the questions that follow. Use the space below and on the next page for your notes.

Here are some words and definitions you will need to know as you read or listen to the myths:

"Why the Fawn Has Spots"

• **trait:** part of one's character; a quality or characteristic like kindness or selfishness

"Pushing Up the Sky"

• **dissatisfied:** unhappy

• **resolved:** decided

If this is a Listening Session, your teacher will now give you copies of the two myths. By studying the myths, the *Strategies and Tips*, and the sample answers, you will learn how to become a better listener and reader.

Strategies and Tips for Listening

• Determine your purpose for listening. Listen carefully as your teacher reads the brief introduction to each myth. Are you listening to remember facts and detailed information, or are you listening to make inferences and draw conclusions from a story that has characters, setting, and action? **Setting a purpose** for listening will help you get the most from the story you hear.

• Listen for **main ideas** and **details** that support those ideas.

• Let your **imagination** help you. As you hear the story, try to visualize the setting, characters, and action. You will remember more information if you let your mind create images.

• Finally, **listen carefully** as your teacher reads. Ignore any distractions around you.

INSTRUCTION

Strategies and Tips for Note Taking

- The second time you listen to the myths read aloud, you will take notes. Taking notes helps you remember information, organize it, and use it to help you answer the questions that follow the stories.
- Use the **5Ws** and **H** to help you take notes. Think of the *who, what, when, where, why* and *how* as questions. Your notes are the **answers** to these questions.
- Use your **own words** to write your notes. Keep your notes as **brief** as possible. Use **short phrases** instead of complete sentences. Often, it is helpful to use a graphic organizer, such as a web or cluster map, a chart, or an outline.
- Use **symbols** or **abbreviations** when you can. For example, use *w/* for *with*; & for *and*; = for *equals*.

Notes

Sample Notes

creation myths = origin tales—attempt to explain natural events and help people make sense of world.

"Why the Fawn Has Spots"	"Pushing Up the Sky"
Who or **what** is story about? explains why fawn is given spots	**Who** or **what** is story about? explains why sky is the height it is today
What event happened? Wakan Takan—Great One—gave animals special trait, but not fawn	**What** event happened? Great Creator (like Wakan Takan) made sky too low
When did event happen? long, long ago	**When** did event happen? long, long ago
Where did event happen? when W.T. created world	**Where** did event happen? when Great Creator created world
Why did something happen? mother deer asks W. T. why fawn has no special trait = protection from enemies. Other animals do—mountain lion = sharp claws; grizzly bear = claws; birds = flight	**Why** did something happen? G.C. made sky too low—tall people bump heads
How story ended or how **problem** was solved: W. T. gives fawn spots (camouflage) so enemies can't see her.	**How story** ended or how **problem** was solved? people—all different languages. Solution: people work as one. Agree to word "Yaa-uhh!" People in west cry "Yaa-uhh!" and everyone in world pushes up sky.

➡ **REMINDER** By turning the **5Ws** and **H** into questions, you have listed all the main ideas and the details that support those ideas.

Stop

©2002 Options Publishing, Inc.

No copying permitted.

26 Using specific details from the myth, complete the chart below to show what Wakan Takan gave to each animal.

Strategies and Tips for Identifying Supporting Details

- Imagine that you say to your parents, "I need a new computer." Without adding some **details** that **support** your main idea, you might not get very far. But what if you said, "I need a new computer. My old one doesn't have enough memory to run my new programs, and the hard drive is too small—it's full. At the computer club in school, we are getting ready to enter the state programming competition. That means I'll have to do a lot of work at home." These supporting details give solid reasons as to why you need a new computer—and they might help to convince your parents! Main ideas are not very meaningful *unless* they are supported by details.
- In "Why the Fawn Has Spots," one main idea is to explain an event in nature—why animals have certain traits or characteristics. The details in the story should support that main idea.

Sample Response

Animal	Gift
mountain lion	sharp claws
grizzly bear	sharp teeth
birds	ability to fly
deer	speed
rabbits	speed
	Complete and accurate notes.

➡ **REMINDER** The specific details—the special traits given to each animal—support, or build on, the main idea, which explains *why* the animals are given special traits.

TRY IT! On the lines below, make a list of the special traits, or characteristics, that cats have.

_____

_____

_____

INSTRUCTION

©2002 Options Publishing, Inc.

Go on

27 Explain how the special gifts that Wakan Takan gave to each animal helped it to survive. Use information from the myth to support your answer.

Strategies and Tips for Linking Main Ideas and Supporting Details

- In Number 26, you found specific details about what gifts Wakan Takan gave each animal. Now you are asked to explain how those gifts helped each animal to survive.
- The first step in answering Number 27 is to look back at your notes. Notice that under the heading "why," you have listed that other animals were given gifts, or traits, for protection. The bear's sharp claws, the mountain lion's sharp teeth, the bird's ability to fly, and the deer and rabbits great speed are traits that protect the animals.

Sample Response   *good details for support*

Wakan Takan, the Great One, gave each animal a special trait that would protect it from its enemies and help it to survive. Wakan Takan gave the mountain lion sharp claws and the bear sharp teeth. These gifts help the animals protect themselves. The birds can escape by flying away. The deer and rabbits were given great speed to escape from their enemies.

TRY IT! Now you will link main ideas and supporting details. Using the details you have listed in the **TRY IT!** on page 101, explain how a cat's characteristics help it to survive.

_____

_____

_____

_____

_____

_____

©2002 Options Publishing, Inc.

28 What natural event does "Pushing Up the Sky" attempt to explain? Use details from the myth to support your answer.

Strategies and Tips for Identifying Supporting Details

- **Supporting details** give you specific information that supports the main idea of a story.
- The first step in using supporting details in your answer is to determine the **main idea** of the story. In Number 28, you are asked to identify the main idea: What natural event "Pushing Up the Sky" explains. The story explains *why the sky is the height it is today.*
- Now you need to look for details in the story that support that main idea. Ask yourself, "What details led me to conclude that the story was about the origin of why the sky is so high?" Make a list of details:
  - sky too low—tall people kept bumping their heads
  - the people were unhappy with that
  - the people got together, yelled the same word, and pushed up the sky

Sample Response

good text support

"Pushing Up the Sky" is a creation myth that attempts to explain the origin of the sky and why it is the height it is today. The Great Creator made the people and the sky. The people were unhappy with the sky because it was too low. Tall people kept bumping their heads against the sky. All the people got together. When the people in the west yelled, "Yaa-uhh!" everyone pushed the sky up to its present height.

➡ **REMINDER** All the supporting details listed in the box above are used in the answer.

TRY IT! Now think of two more new supporting details that you could *add* to your myth about cats. On the lines below, write your answer.

_____

_____

©2002 Options Publishing, Inc.

No copying permitted.

Go on

INSTRUCTION

Planning Page

PLAN your writing for Number 29 here, but do NOT write your final answer on this page.
This page is for your use only. Your writing on this Planning Page will NOT count toward your final score. **Write your final answer on the next page.**

Answer

Strategies and Tips for Outlining

- One of the best ways to plan your writing is to make an **outline**. Roman numerals (I., II.), letters, and Arabic numerals (1., 2.) are used to show main ideas and supporting details.

- By dividing your ideas into main ideas and supporting details, you will find that your writing is organized and your ideas are connected.

Here is an example of an outline used to organize facts for Number 29. The topic is creation myths.

I. *Comparison of types of events* (**main idea**)
  A. Both are creation myths (origin tales) (**first important subtopic**)
  B. Both explain how a natural event occurred (**second important subtopic**)

II. *Descriptions of what each myth explains* (**main idea**)
  A. Fawn (**subtopic**)
    1. Explains why fawn is born with spots (**supporting detail**)
    2. Problem: fawn was not protected from enemies (**supporting detail**)
    3. Solution: fawn given spots when born to camouflage it from enemies (**supporting detail**)
  B. Sky (**subtopic**)
    1. Explains why sky is so high (**supporting detail**)
    2. Problem: sky too low for tall people (**supporting detail**)
    3. Solution: people work together to push up sky (**supporting detail**)

III. *Why people told creation myths* (**main idea**)
  A. People are curious about why natural events occur and ask questions (**subtopic**)
    1. Why is the fawn born with spots but adult deer do not have spots (**supporting detail**)
    2. Why can a person climb the highest mountain or tree and still not reach the top of the sky (**supporting detail**)
  B. People needed reasons for why natural events occurred—helped people to make sense of the world around them (**subtopic**)

always go back to text for details

➡ **REMINDER** In Number 29, you are asked to include these main ideas: *comparison of the natural events, descriptions of the events,* and *why you think people told creation myths.* Note that the Roman numerals match the main ideas you must include in your essay.

©2002 Options Publishing, Inc.

No copying permitted.

29 Discuss why these stories are called creation myths.

In your discussion, be sure to include
- a description of what these myths are called and why
- a comparison of the types of natural events explained
- why you think people told creation myths

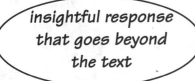 Check your writing for correct spelling, grammar, paragraphs, and punctuation.

Strategies and Tips for Writing
- Now it is time to turn your outline into an essay.
- The first step is to look at your outline and the three main ideas listed for Roman numerals I., II., and III. Each main idea becomes a paragraph. Each main idea also becomes the **topic sentence**—a sentence that states the main idea of a paragraph—for each paragraph. Notice that in the answer below, each topic sentence is in boldfaced type.
- Notice also that all the other sentences in the paragraphs are **details** that support the topic sentences.

Sample Response

   Both "Why the Fawn Has Spots" and "Pushing Up the Sky" are creation myths. Creation myths attempt to explain the origins of events that occur in nature.

   "Why the Fawn Has Spots" tries to explain why deer are given camouflage spots when they are fawns. Wakan Takan gave the fawn a spotted coat. These spots help the fawn to blend in with the ground and hide it from its enemies. **"Pushing Up the Sky" attempts to explain how the sky was made and why it is so high.** In the beginning of the world, the Great Creator made the sky too low. Tall people bumped their heads against it. All the people worked together to push up the sky.

   People probably told creation myths to explain how and why events in nature happened. People wondered why a fawn has spots, but an adult deer does not. When people climbed mountains or trees, they probably wondered why they could not reach the top of the sky. These myths helped people to make sense of the world around them.

insightful response that goes beyond the text

thorough understanding of text

INSTRUCTION

©2002 Options Publishing, Inc.

Go on

TRY IT! You have already listed the special traits that a cat has, and you have explained how these traits help it to survive. Plan your own creation myth that explains *how* and *why* cats were given these special characteristics.

- First, make an outline of your ideas in the space below.
- Then use the outline to write *your* creation myth on the lines below.

Outline:

_____

_____

_____

_____

_____

_____

_____

_____

_____

_____

Essay:

_____

_____

_____

_____

_____

_____

_____

_____

_____

_____

_____

_____

Stop

No copying permitted.

© Educational Options Publishing, Inc.

Directions

Here is the article "The Italian Granite Worker" and the poem "Life" that appeared in Test A. Read the article and the poem again, and then compare *your* answers with the answers given here. Read *Strategies and Tips* to learn how to find the correct answers, and use the *TRY IT!* activities for additional practice.

Now begin reading.

The Italian Granite Worker

This story is based on interviews conducted with Giacomo Coletti as part of the Federal Writers' Project 1936-1940.

The shrill alarm clock breaks the silence of the bleak February morning in 1939. Almost instantly Giacomo Coletti reaches across the bed and turns the alarm off before it wakes his wife, Nina. Dawn has not yet broken, but it is time to get up for work. He begins every morning trying to clear the granite dust that has settled in his throat and lungs.

Giacomo has worked in the granite sheds (the buildings where the stone is cut, carved, and sculpted) since he arrived in the United States from Italy more than 20 years ago. As the years pass, the coughing spells last longer and longer.

Giacomo's eldest son, Giorgio, hears his father's cough. He, like his father, works in the sheds. He worries about his father's health as well as his own. In an attempt to breath as much fresh air as possible, Giorgio sleeps with his windows open even during the harsh New England winters.

Giacomo is well aware of the dangers of working in the granite sheds. Today, they will bury his good friend Pietro. He died of tuberculosis, which is a lung disease. Giacomo recalls with a twinge of guilt the letter he wrote to Pietro, convincing Pietro to leave Italy and join him in Vermont. Pietro was a dear friend. It was Pietro who escorted Giacomo's wife, Nina, across the Atlantic Ocean to the United States.

©2002 Options Publishing, Inc.

Nina tries to convince her husband that it is not his fault. She says that it was Pietro's time to die—whether he lived in Italy, Africa, or Montpelier, Vermont.

Giacomo and his Italian, Scottish, Scandinavian, Spanish, and French co-workers will put in a full day's work before they visit Pietro's home. The sheds are grim and gray. Spurts of steam escape from the chimneys. But Giacomo chooses to think of the satisfaction and joy he finds from turning a piece of stone into a beautiful carving.

Inside, Giacomo begins his work. Today, he is carving an angel on a tombstone for a young child who has passed away. He works hard to capture the right look of innocence and joy in the **cherub's** eyes. Giacomo takes special care with this project—he knows the young boy's father.

cherub: an angel usually portrayed as chubby and childlike

At lunchtime, Giacomo and Giorgio make their way home—happy to be free of the **confining** sheds. Nina has prepared their favorite Italian foods for the midday meal. Giacomo and Giorgio also enjoy the many new recipes Nina has learned from her American-born neighbors.

confining: limiting; small and crowded

©2002 Options Publishing, Inc.

No copying permitted.

After work, Giacomo laughs and jokes with his friends. But in the back of his mind, he is thinking about his friend, Pietro, who is not there—the friend he will say good-bye to tonight.

Pietro's home is crowded with granite workers and their families. Eventually the women return home and the men take turns sitting with Pietro. Each time a man coughs or wheezes a tense silence falls on the room. The men wonder to themselves who will be the next to follow Pietro to an early grave.

Years ago, Nina tried to convince Giacomo to find a different line of work. But he never wanted his family to suffer financially. He wanted to feed his children and pay his bills. Giacomo could not take time off to find a new job. Instead, he accepted the fact that the granite dust he breathed in every day might shorten his life. He is too old now to learn a new trade. Besides, he has come to love and appreciate the beauty of granite. Giacomo takes pride in the sculptures he makes. He is proud that his hands create the monuments that keep alive the memory of those, like Pietro, who went before him.

©2002 Options Publishing, Inc.

INSTRUCTION

Go on

No copying permitted.

30 Complete the chart with words or phrases that describe Giacomo Coletti's character. Identify information from the article that supports each character trait.

Sample Response *complete and accurate chart*

Character Trait	Supporting Information
Responsible or Reliable	Made sure that family never suffered financially; supports family despite the risks to his health by working in the granite sheds
Thoughtful or Considerate	He takes special care with the cherub he is carving for a young boy's grave—he knows the father and feels sympathetic; turns off alarm clock before it wakes up his wife
Talented or Skilled	He creates beautiful granite monuments. He takes pride in his sculptures (like the cherub).

Strategies and Tips for Understanding Character Traits

- **Character traits** are the qualities that make up a person's personality.
- You probably know people who are cheerful and upbeat, people who are somber or serious, or people who are generous or miserly. You decide what qualities, or character traits, people have by listening to their words and statements and observing their actions.
- In literature, you learn about a character's traits almost the same way. You read what he or she says, what he or she does, or what he or she thinks. A character's words, actions, and thoughts reinforce, or support, that character trait.

TRY IT! Look at the supporting information for each of Giacomo's character traits in Number 30. Next to each character trait listed below, explain how you learned about that character trait—through his *words, actions,* or *thoughts.*

1. Responsible: _____

2. Thoughtful: _____

3. Talented: _____

©2002 Options Publishing, Inc.

No copying permitted.

31 How does Giacomo Coletti feel about his job in the granite sheds? Explain your answer using details from the article.

good supporting details

Sample Response

Giacomo Coletti knew that the job in the granite sheds was unhealthy for his lungs. But he loved his family and did not want to take time off to look for a new job. He did not want his family to suffer financially. Despite the risks to his health, Giacomo is proud of his skill and the beautiful monuments he creates.

Strategies and Tips for Making Inferences About Character Traits

- An **inference** is a conclusion you make based on specific facts. You can often make an inference about a character's personality from details given in the selection. These details may come from the character's thoughts, words, or actions.

➡ **REMINDER** By examining Giacomo's feelings about his job, you can infer that two of his character traits are responsibility (to his family) and pride in his accomplishments (he is proud of his talent).

TRY IT! What can you infer about Giacomo's personality from this quotation from the article: "Giacomo recalls with a twinge of guilt the letter he wrote to Pietro, convincing Pietro to leave Italy and join him in Vermont . . . It was Pietro who escorted Giacomo's wife, Nina, across the Atlantic Ocean to the United States"? Write your answer on the lines below.

_____

_____

_____

_____

©2002 Options Publishing, Inc.

No copying permitted.

INSTRUCTION

Go on

Life

Paul Laurence Dunbar

A crust of bread and a corner to sleep in,

A minute to smile and an hour to weep in,

A pint of joy to a peck of trouble,

And never a laugh but the moans come double:

　　And that is life!

A crust and a corner that love makes precious,

With the smile to warm and the tears to refresh us;

And joys seem sweeter when cares come after,

And a moan is the finest of **foils** for laughter:

　　And that is life!

> **pint of joy to a peck of trouble:** a pint is two cups; a peck is eight quarts or 32 cups

> **foils:** a person or thing that sets off or increases the value of another by contrast; to serve as a contrast to

©2002 Options Publishing, Inc.

No copying permitted.

32 What is most likely the poet's purpose in writing this poem? Use ideas from the poem to support your answer.

good choice of line for support

Sample Response

The poem's purpose is to get people to treasure the good times in their lives. Dunbar says that "joys seem sweeter when cares come after." He is saying that the hard times in life make the better times even more special.

Strategies and Tips for Identifying the Author's Purpose

• To identify an **author's purpose**, ask yourself: What is the author's general objective—how does the author want me to respond? What specific ideas does the author what me to understand?

• The **general purpose** might be to entertain, to persuade, to inform, to explain, or to describe. The **specific purpose** is tied to the theme. The specific purpose is the main point the author wants to make about the topic.

TRY IT! To help determine the poet's purpose, answer these questions:

1. How does the poet want me to respond? _____

_____

2. What specific ideas does the poet want to convey to me? _____

_____

3. What is the poet's attitude, or feelings, toward the subject? _____

_____

INSTRUCTION

Go on

©2002 Options Publishing, Inc.

No copying permitted.

Planning Page

PLAN your writing for Number 33 here, but do NOT write your final answer on this page. *This page is for your use only. Your writing on this Planning Page will NOT count toward your final score.* Write your final answer beginning on the next page.

Strategies and Tips for Applying Themes

- A **theme** is a central message or purpose of a selection. A theme is often expressed as a general statement about human nature or about life.
- The first step in planning your answer for Number 33 is to make sure that you understand the themes, or messages, in "The Italian Granite Worker" and "Life." To discover the theme of a story or a poem, think about the feelings you have *as* you read the selections and *after* you read them. Ask yourself these questions: Did the events or images remind me of things that have happened in my life or the life of someone I know? What do the two selections tell me about human nature or life?
- Finally, look for details in the selection that support the theme.

Sample Notes

Here is one way to organize your thoughts:

Theme

Supporting Lines

Details from Article

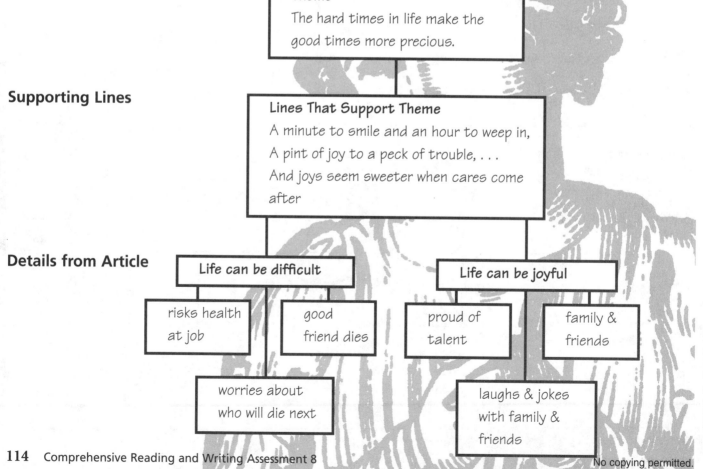

Theme
The hard times in life make the good times more precious.

Lines That Support Theme
A minute to smile and an hour to weep in,
A pint of joy to a peck of trouble, . . .
And joys seem sweeter when cares come after

Life can be difficult
- risks health at job
- good friend dies
- worries about who will die next

Life can be joyful
- proud of talent
- family & friends
- laughs & jokes with family & friends

©2002 Options Publishing, Inc.

No copying permitted.

33 Choose a line or lines from the poem. Discuss the meaning of your selection, and explain how it applies to Giacomo Coletti. Use ideas from BOTH the poem and the article in your answer.

In your answer, be sure to include

- the line or lines you have selected from the poem
- an explanation of how your selection applies to Giacomo Coletti

Check your writing for correct spelling, grammar, paragraphs, and punctuation.

good choice of lines from poem

Sample Response

The poem "Life," by Paul Laurence Dunbar, relates to the granite worker Giacomo Coletti. The lines that especially relate are these: "A minute to smile and an hour to weep in, A pint of joy to a peck of trouble. . . . And joys seem sweeter when cares come after." These lines relate to Giacomo. He stays at a job that is dangerous to his health because he loves his family and never wants them to suffer. He also sees the things in life that give him joy. His family and friends give him joy, and he is proud of the monuments he creates. Even though he has more hard and sad times in life than good times, he appreciates what he does have. Giacomo would probably agree with this line from the poem, "And that is life!"

support shows thorough understanding of text

TRY IT! Reorganize the ideas you wrote about for Number 33 on page 29 by using the Main Idea/Supporting Details graphic organizer on the next page.

INSTRUCTION

Go on

Main Idea/Supporting Details

Theme

Your Supporting Lines

Details from Article

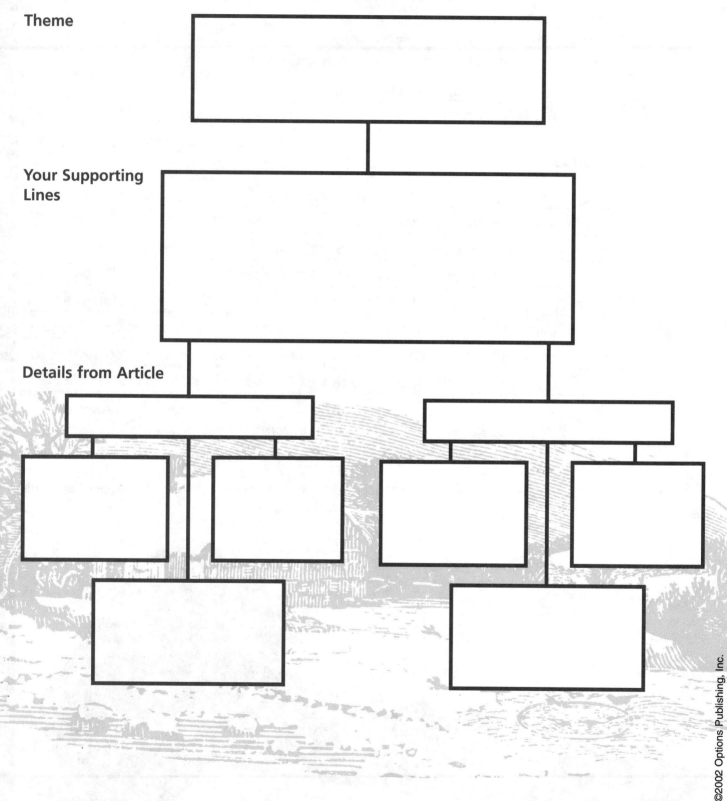

©2002 Options Publishing, Inc.

No copying permitted.

Planning Page

PLAN your writing for Number 34 here, but do NOT write your final answer on this page. *This page is for your use only. Your writing on this Planning Page will NOT count toward your final score.* Write your final answer beginning on the next page.

Answer →

> ### Strategies and Tips for Outlining/Writing
> • Outlining helps you formally organize your ideas, but a **basic outline pattern** also provides a helpful form in which to write down your ideas as you think of them. Start by the main ideas listed in Number 34. Under each main idea, jot down supporting details.
> • Notice that the main ideas listed in Number 34 are written as questions on this Planning Page.

Sample Response

I. **Introduction:** *Who* is the person and *what* did the person do?
   - Person is my aunt
   - Very talented—artist, musician, writer, athlete
   - Aunt helps people who lost eyesight to lead independent and fulfilling lives

II. **Body:** *What* difficulties in life did he or she face?
   - Aunt lost eyesight at 19 & at that time (1965) no laws to protect disabled
   - No opportunities. Discriminated against in employment and education
   - Colleges told aunt that they could not accommodate person with handicap
   - No employment agency would take aunt as client
   - Little help from state—they suggested she live in institution and sell light bulbs

III. **Body:** *Why* does the person take pride in his or her accomplishments?
   - Persevered her dream of going to college—got permission to tape-record professors' lectures & then types her notes in Braille
   - Started dept. in college that helps people w/ disabilities—people volunteered to record "talking textbooks"

IV. **Conclusion:** Summarize the results of the person's goals
   Helped change the way people think about blind
   - Dedicated life to help blind people pursue their dreams—jobs & education
   - Found joy in life. Chooses to look at positive side of life and not her difficulties

©2002 Options Publishing, Inc.

Go on

TRY IT! On the lines below, rewrite the notes *you* made for *your* essay topic. Use the notes you wrote for the Planning Page on page 32. Put your notes into the basic outline pattern you read about on page 117.

_____

_____

_____

_____

_____

_____

_____

_____

_____

_____

_____

_____

_____

_____

_____

_____

_____

_____

_____

_____

_____

_____

_____

_____

©2002 Options Publishing, Inc.

No copying permitted.

34 Both "An Italian Granite Worker" and "Life" describe life as a mixture of hard times and good times. Write an essay about a person in history or someone *you* know who has experienced difficult times but still appreciates life and takes pride in his or her accomplishments.

In your essay, be sure to include

- who the person is
- what he or she did
- the difficulties he or she faced
- why the person takes pride in his or her accomplishments
- an introduction, a body, and a conclusion

Check your writing for correct spelling, grammar, paragraphs, and punctuation.

You've answered all aspects of the question.

Sample Response

The person I know who has experienced difficult times in life is my aunt. But she continues to appreciate the positive things in life and her accomplishments. She is a talented artist, musician, and writer. My aunt has also dedicated her life to helping people who have lost their eyesight. She knows the importance of leading an independent and satisfying life.

In 1965, when my aunt was nineteen years old, she lost her eyesight. At that time, there were very few laws to protect or to guarantee the rights of disabled people. They were discriminated against in employment and education. My aunt found that she had very few opportunities. Colleges returned her applications saying that they could not accommodate people with disabilities. Employment agencies said that they could not help her find a job because none were available for a blind person. Even the state suggested that she move to an institution and think about selling light bulbs.

Despite everyone's negative outlook, my aunt convinced a local college to let her try one semester. She got permission to tape-record the professors' lectures. Then she listened to the tape and took notes in Braille. She also helped the college set up a department to help people with disabilities. Volunteers read the textbooks onto a tape so that blind students could listen to books necessary for their courses. By the end of the semester, my aunt received an A in every course.

Good use of supporting details.

Go on

©2002 Options Publishing, Inc.

No copying permitted.

INSTRUCTION

My aunt now works for the state, teaching those who have lost their eyesight how to cook for themselves and their families, how to go shopping, and how to succeed in school. Both her attitude toward life and her dedication to her job have helped to change the way people think about the blind. Although she faces many difficulties, my aunt has always looked at the joys in life, and she continues to pursue her goals.

Conclusion goes beyond question— shows insight.

TRY IT!   In the **TRY IT!** on page 116, you reorganized the notes you made for the topic *you chose* to write about for Number 34. You probably have more information, or that information is better organized. Now that you have reorganized your notes with added information, rewrite your essay on the lines below. Be sure that you include an introduction, a body, and a conclusion in your essay.

When you are finished, exchange your essay with a classmate's. Using what you have learned about organizing ideas for writing, comment on each other's essays.

_____

_____

_____

_____

_____

_____

_____

_____

_____

_____

_____

_____

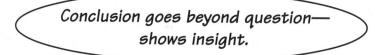

Stop

©2002 Options Publishing, Inc.

No copying permitted.

You have already completed Test B on pages 35 through 66. The following pages reproduce Test B, but this time you will learn why specific multiple-choice answers are correct or incorrect. You will also learn about how to become a better listener and writer.

By reading these pages and completing the exercises, you will learn strategies that will help you take tests, understand what you hear, and improve your writing skills.

The following test will help you master important reading, thinking, and writing skills:

- **Reading Session:** Each multiple-choice question is labeled with the *type* of skill it teaches. You will also learn how to choose the correct answer by reading why each answer is correct or incorrect. You will learn **Strategies and Tips** for answering the questions. And you will practice what you have learned about each skill with a **TRY IT!** activity.

- **Reading and Listening Session:** In this part of the test, you read two selections or listened as your teacher read the two selections aloud to you. On the following pages, you will learn how to take notes about the most important details and ideas in the selections. You will also learn how to understand and explain those important ideas by organizing your thoughts *before* you write your answers. By using the **Strategies and Tips** in this part of the test, you will learn how to become a better listener, reader, note-taker, and writer. Use the **TRY IT!** activities to practice the skills you have learned.

- **Writing Session:** In this part of the test, you will learn **Strategies and Tips** for finding supporting details, understanding diagrams, and organizing your writing by using an outline. Use the **TRY IT!** activities to sharpen your thinking and writing skills.

Directions for Reading Session

In this part of the test, you will read two articles and a story. As you answer the questions about what you have read, you may look back at the reading selections as often as you like.

Now begin reading.

©2002 Options Publishing, Inc.

Directions

Here is the article "Stranded in Antarctica" that appeared in Test B. Reread the article, and then compare *your* answers with the answers given here. Read *Strategies and Tips* to learn how to find the correct answer, and use the *TRY IT!* activities for additional practice.

STRANDED IN ANTARCTICA

"Abandon ship!" Shackleton shouted out. It was October 27, 1915, and with this command, Ernest Shackleton knew he had also abandoned his dream to be the first to walk across the continent of Antarctica. He also knew that survival on the frozen sea was almost impossible. It was 1915, and there were no radios, telephones, or high-tech tools for navigation. The crew scrambled to get food, gear, and the lifeboats off the ship. They would need these small boats if they hoped to survive.

The *Endurance* trapped in the ice pack.

A year earlier, Shackleton's trip began well enough. The British eagerly supported and financed the expedition. Yet Shackleton knew it would not be an easy trip. In Antarctica, the winter temperature can drop to 100° below zero Fahrenheit as winter winds race across the ice at 200 miles per hour. Shackleton hired an experienced crew and planned the expedition for the spring, when weather conditions were a little better.

On August 1, 1914, *Endurance* and its crew left the dock in London, and by October they arrived in Buenos Aires, on the coast of Argentina. Here, they picked up the sled dogs, and on November 5, the ship landed at the whaling town on South Georgia Island, located southeast off the tip of South America. Because the seasons are reversed in the Southern Hemisphere, spring was under way. The plan was to leave immediately for Antarctica; however, a severe, brutal winter delayed the voyage. Ice still choked most of the Weddell Sea, just north of Antarctica. Another tedious

©2002 Options Publishing, Inc.

Shackleton and the crew dragging a lifeboat across the ice.

month passed until, finally, on December 5, *Endurance* set sail for the southern continent.

The men had never seen so much ice, and they lost precious months picking their way through icebergs. By January 19, 1915, the ship was still 100 miles from the continent, but the frozen Weddell Sea surrounded *Endurance* on all sides, and the ice pack was drifting northward, taking the ship with it.

Shackleton soon realized that they would spend the winter trapped on the ship. Howling blizzards overwhelmed the men as they worked day and night chipping away at the ice crushing the ship. It was a hopeless battle—the boards on deck twisted, and the ship's hull sprang leaks. Shackleton wrote in his diary, "It was a sickening sensation to feel the decks breaking up under one's feet, the great beams bending and then snapping with a noise like gun-fire." On October 27, 1915, Shackleton ordered the crew to abandon the ship. Soon after, the ice crushed *Endurance* and it sank. Now the men and their supplies stood on the frozen sea; however, it was spring in Antarctica, and the shifting ice pack could suddenly break apart under their feet. If the men did not move soon, none would survive.

Shackleton and the men decided to haul the supplies and lifeboats across the frozen sea to Paulet Island, 346 miles to the northwest. Dragging the boats was grueling. The ice was in jagged pieces, and the men often had to lift the boats over waves frozen in midair. But the boats were necessary. Soon, the crew hoped, they would reach open water—and home.

Go on

©2002 Options Publishing, Inc.

Shackleton's challenge was to hold the twenty-seven men together—without one another, they would all die. They must make open water before the soft ice crumbled beneath them. Finally, on March 9, 1916, the men felt the swell of the ocean beneath the ice pack. They were 30 miles from the open ocean. A month later, the sea opened, and Shackleton gave orders to launch the boats. The voyagers had marched 600 backbreaking miles since the ice first trapped *Endurance*. They had risked starvation, drowning, and freezing to death.

The men rowed with all their remaining strength, struggling to avoid icebergs. As night came, the exhausted crew looked for a firm ice pack to camp. Fortunately, apprehension kept Shackleton awake. During the night, he left his tent and watched in horror as the ice pack suddenly cracked under the men's tent! The men quickly pulled one another from the tent.

"Launch the boats!" Shackleton yelled. Men grabbed instruments, gear, and food as they tried to outrun the cracking ice. Once in the boats, Frank Worsley, the navigator and captain, set a course to Elephant Island.

On April 15, the half-frozen men landed on Elephant Island—solid land at last! Yet they knew they could not survive the winter on this barren, wind-blown island. Someone had to get help—and that help was at the whaling town on South Georgia Island, 800 miles to the east. Nine days later, Shackleton and five of the crew took a lifeboat and set off. It was a miserable journey as terrifying gales blew the ship off course and waves soaked the men.

Subzero temperatures froze their clothing. Sleep was impossible. Everyone suffered from frostbite. Seventeen agonizing days later, the men landed on the island, but they had one last ordeal to overcome. The whaling town was on the other side of the island, and *no one* had ever crossed the island's mountain range. It was a tremendous risk, but Shackleton knew it was his only hope of saving the men.

On May 18, Shackleton and two of the crew set off. Exhausted, they reached the summit and pressed on. Finally, they saw the town before them. As they staggered into the factory manager's house, they knew the rescue of the entire crew was now certain.

Unbelievably, Shackleton and the crew of twenty-seven men all lived. With Shackleton's leadership, they managed to survive by using courage, strength, and teamwork.

©2002 Options Publishing, Inc.

    No copying permitted.

Question 1   This question is about **identifying the author's purpose** for writing. The *author's purpose* is the reason he or she wrote the selection.

 Strategies and Tips for Identifying the Author's Purpose

An author usually has two purposes for writing—a **general purpose** and a **specific purpose**. Knowing an author's purpose helps you judge the writer and the selection fairly.

- The **general purpose** might be to entertain, to persuade, to inform, to explain, or to describe. "Stranded in Antarctica" *describes* the Shackleton expedition.

- The **specific purpose** is tied to the theme of the selection and is the main point the author wants to make about the topic. Often, the author reinforces the specific purpose in the closing paragraph of the article. The theme is expressed in the last paragraph of the article: "With Shackleton's leadership, they managed to survive by using courage, strength, and teamwork."

1   **What is the author's purpose in writing this article?**

  Ⓐ to entertain readers with an amusing story   **Incorrect.** The men's struggle for survival is not humorous.

  Ⓑ to explain how and why the *Endurance* sank   **Incorrect.** This is not the author's main purpose. This is just one of the events that happened.

  Ⓒ to describe how Shackleton and the men survived being stranded in Antarctica   **Correct. This is the *author's main purpose*. The article focuses on the men's struggle for survival and Shackleton's leadership.**

  Ⓓ to persuade others to explore the South Pole   **Incorrect.** There is nothing in the article that attempts to persuade others to explore the South Pole.

TRY IT!   To help identify the author's purpose for writing, answer the following questions.

1. What specific, or main, point does the author want to communicate?

_____

_____

2. How does the author want me to respond after reading the article about Shackleton?

_____

_____

INSTRUCTION

Go on

©2002 Options Publishing, Inc.

Question 2   This question is about **identifying the genre** of a selection. The *genre* identifies the type of literary work, such as nonfiction, fiction, poetry, and drama. Each genre has its own unique characteristics.

Strategies and Tips for Identifying Genre

Literary **genre** refers to the type of literature you read.

- **Fiction** is writing that uses characters and events that are not real. Myths, folktales, and many short stories are fiction.

- **Nonfiction** is writing that uses people, places, and events that are real. Articles, essays, biographies, autobiographies, and profiles are all nonfiction. They are about real people, places, or events.

- "Stranded in Antarctica" is an article. **Articles** inform or explain a subject to readers and are generally found in newspapers and magazines. Articles usually present facts rather than opinions.

2   "Stranded in Antarctica" is an article because it is a work of

(F)   nonfiction that tries to persuade a reader to think a certain way.

Incorrect. An essay typically tries to persuade a reader to act or think a certain way.

(G)   fiction that has characters and events that are not real.

Incorrect. Articles are about real people and real events.

(H)   nonfiction that is written by a person about his or her own life.

Incorrect. This answer describes an autobiography.

(J)   nonfiction that gives the reader facts about a subject.

Correct. This article gives you facts about the Shackleton expedition.

TRY IT!   Review the definition of an article in the **Strategies and Tips** box above. Then describe two characteristics in "Stranded in Antarctica" that show it is an article.

1. _____

_____

_____

_____

2. _____

_____

_____

_____

     No copying permitted.

©2002 Options Publishing, Inc.

Question 3
This question is about **drawing conclusions**. *Drawing conclusions* means making judgments based only on the *facts* that are presented in the selection.

Strategies and Tips for Drawing Conclusions

- A conclusion is never a wild guess. A **conclusion** is a decision or opinion that you make based on the *facts* that you have read.
- Make sure that the facts in the selection support your conclusion. For example: *Chris walks home from school every day. He takes the bus only when it rains* (facts). *This afternoon, Chris took the bus home* (fact). You can logically conclude from the *facts* that it must have rained this afternoon.

3 You can draw the conclusion that the members of the crew most likely

Ⓐ were unhappy with Shackleton's leadership.

Incorrect. The article does not give any facts or evidence to support this conclusion.

Ⓑ were experienced sailors.

Correct. You know that Shackleton hired an experienced crew. You can logically conclude that they must have been familiar with boats and rowing because they did survive.

Ⓒ looked forward to the challenge of rowing to Paulet Island.

Incorrect. The article never directly addresses the men's feelings about their experiences.

Ⓓ were surprised that Shackleton returned to rescue them from Elephant Island.

Incorrect. The article does not mention what the men remaining on the island thought.

TRY IT! List two facts from the article that support this conclusion: *Shackleton was an effective and determined leader.* Skim the article for the facts.

1. _____

_____

_____

2. _____

_____

_____

INSTRUCTION

Go on

Question 4   This question is about **making inferences**. *Inferences* are logical guesses based on the evidence and details in the selection.

Strategies and Tips for Making Inferences

- When you do not have enough *facts* to lead you to a conclusion, you make an **inference**—a logical guess—from the details and information you are given. Writers often expect readers to make inferences. Authors do not always tell you what every character is feeling or why something has happened. You must infer what the writer has not directly stated by carefully examining the clues and details in a selection. When you make an inference, use the details from the story along with your knowledge and common sense about life.

- Read this sentence: *Jamal left the hospital wearing a white lab coat and a name badge.* You can logically infer that Jamal works at the hospital—but you must not assume too much. You *cannot* infer that Jamal is a doctor or a nurse. He might work as a lab assistant.

4   **In 1914, the expedition had to wait an extra month at South Georgia Island before leaving for the Antarctic because the winter was so severe. You can infer that the winter of 1914 was unusually harsh because**

(F) they enjoyed their stopover at South Georgia Island and decided to stay longer.

Incorrect. There are no details in the article to support this inference. It also does not explain why the winter was unusually harsh.

(G) the expedition had to wait for the sled dogs to arrive.

Incorrect. You cannot support this from the details in the article.

(H) Shackleton would not have left if he thought the ship would become trapped in ice.

Correct. It is logical to infer that Shackleton would not have risked the expedition if he thought that this particular winter was unusually severe. Use the evidence in the article, your knowledge, and your common sense to make inferences.

(J) the seasons are reversed in the Southern Hemisphere.

Incorrect. This has nothing to do with the harshness of the winters in Antarctica.

TRY IT! Imagine that you are with your parents and you visit one of their friends for the first time. When you walk into the house, you see a bowl of dog food on the floor and a leash hanging from a hook in the kitchen. Circle the letter of the correct inference below. Then explain why that inference is correct and the other is incorrect.

A. Your parents' friends own a dog.

B. Your parents' friends have a dog in their home.

_____

_____

_____

_____

©2002 Options Publishing, Inc.

No copying permitted.

Question 5   This question is about **identifying details** from the selection. *Details* are the *who, what, when, where, why,* and *how* of what you have read. This type of question checks your basic understanding of the selection.

Strategies and Tips for Identifying Details

- **Details** in a selection help you organize the information that an author gives you. They also help you keep events in order. Details are different from supporting details. Supporting details help develop the main idea. **Details** are the basics—they tell you the **5Ws and H:** the *who, what, when, where, why,* and *How* of a story. Follow these steps to help you remember details:
- After you read the directions and introductory sentence to the selection, take a moment to **predict** what you might learn from the article. When you finish reading the selection, **reflect** on what you have read. **Reread** any parts of the selection that are still unclear.
- Do not reread the entire story to look for details. Always skim the story to find the detail asked in the question.

5   How many miles did the men have to row from Elephant Island to reach South Georgia Island?

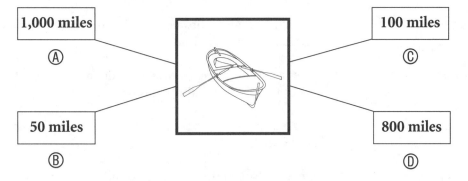

1,000 miles
Ⓐ

50 miles
Ⓑ

100 miles
Ⓒ

800 miles
Ⓓ

Answer D, *800 miles,* is correct.

Answers A, B, and C give the incorrect number of miles. Skim the article to find the correct answer on page 124.

TRY IT! Skim the story to find details about the weather. Then write two details that you learned from the article about the weather conditions in Antarctica.

1. _____

_____

_____

2. _____

_____

_____

©2002 Options Publishing, Inc.

No copying permitted.

Go on

Question 6

This question is about **identifying generalizations**. A *generalization* is a broad statement intended to be true about a group of people, situations, or objects.

Strategies and Tips for Identifying Generalizations

Generalizations *should* be based on facts, but some generalizations are faulty and not based on facts.

- Generalizations are often signaled by clue words: *always, never, all, most,* or *many.* When you read a generalization, evaluate it to see if it is supported by facts, and rely on your own knowledge and experiences.

- A **valid generalization** is *Many birds fly south for the winter.* The key word is *many.* There are several species of birds that migrate south during the winter. If the generalization is supported by facts, it is true, or valid.

- Writers sometimes make errors in reasoning when they try to prove a point. A **faulty generalization** is *All birds fly south for the winter.* If even one type of bird does not fly south, the generalization is faulty. A faulty generalization is untrue because it does not apply to *all* cases.

6 **Which of the following statements is a *valid* generalization?**

Ⓕ Shackleton showed strong leadership qualities throughout the expedition.

Correct. The men followed Shackleton's orders, worked together, and all survived.

Ⓖ All the crew of *Endurance* respected Shackleton.

Incorrect. If even one crewmember did not respect Shackleton, the generalization is faulty.

Ⓗ Sailing for hours on the ocean is a boring task.

Incorrect. This is not valid. Not all people feel this way about sailing.

Ⓙ Anyone can become a member of a wilderness expedition.

Incorrect. Not all people are physically or mentally capable of going on a wilderness expedition.

TRY IT! On the lines below, write your own valid generalization based on events or information in the article. Then list the facts or evidence from the article that support the generalization.

Generalization: _____

_____

_____

Support: _____

_____

©2002 Options Publishing, Inc.

Question 7   This question is about **identifying fact and opinion**. A *fact* can be proved. An *opinion* cannot be proved or disproved. An opinion is based on what someone thinks, feels, or believes.

Strategies and Tips for Identifying Fact and Opinion

- A **fact** is a statement that can be proved. It is supposed to be true or to have really happened. *On August 1, 1914,* Endurance *and its crew left the dock in London* is a fact. You can check a history book or an encyclopedia for this information.

- An **opinion** is a statement about what someone feels or thinks. It cannot be proved or disproved. *It was a miserable journey* is an opinion. The word *miserable* signals a feeling—and feelings are opinions. Words that describe how a person feels or thinks always signal an opinion: *sad, happy, angry, pleased, love, hate, beautiful,* or *wonderful.* An opinion tells what someone feels or believes.

7   Which of the following statements is an opinion?

Ⓐ The men thought the sight of land was beautiful.

Correct. This is an opinion. The men may not have described the barren island as beautiful.

Ⓑ All twenty-seven men survived the expedition to Antarctica.

Incorrect. This is a fact that can be proved. The men did survive.

Ⓒ The ship *Endurance* was crushed by an ice pack.

Incorrect. This is a fact. The article states that the ship was crushed.

Ⓓ Winter temperatures in Antarctica can drop to 100° F. below zero.

Incorrect. This is also a fact. Records of the temperatures in Antarctica prove this statement.

TRY IT! Think about the city or town in which you live. Then write *two* facts and *two* opinions about your town or city.

_____

_____

_____

_____

_____

_____

INSTRUCTION

©2002 Options Publishing, Inc.

No copying permitted.

Go on

Question 8   This question is about understanding a word by **using context clues.** *Context clues* are found in the words and sentences before or after the unfamiliar word. They give clues, or hints, to the meaning of the unfamiliar word.

Strategies and Tips for Using Context Clues

Context clues refer to the words or sentences before or after an unfamiliar word. When you read, authors often use words that are unfamiliar to you. You can frequently determine what that word means by seeing how it is used in the sentence or in the paragraph. Sometimes, authors give you very specific clues:

- **Synonym clue:** A **synonym** is a word that means the same or nearly the same as the unfamiliar word. *Subzero temperatures froze their clothing.* The author provides the synonym *froze* to help you understand the word *subzero.*

- Remember, when you answer multiple-choice questions, be sure to read *all* the choices.

8 The passage states that "a *severe,* brutal winter delayed the voyage."
In this context, the word *severe* means

ⓕ pleasant.   **Incorrect.** This word means the opposite of *severe* and *brutal.*

ⓖ harsh.   **Correct. The author adds the word *brutal* to help you understand the meaning of severe. A *severe* winter is harsh and brutal.**

ⓗ scorching.   **Incorrect.** This does not make sense. It is not scorching, or hot, during the winter.

ⓙ strict.   **Incorrect.** Although this word is a synonym for *severe,* it does not make sense in this sentence. Always read the sentence carefully to find the correct context.

TRY IT! Read these sentences from the article: "Subzero temperatures froze their clothing. Sleep was impossible. Everyone suffered from frostbite. Seventeen *agonizing* days later, the men landed on the island, but they had one last ordeal to overcome." Explain what the word *agonizing* means and what context clues you used to determine that meaning.

_____

_____

_____

©2002 Options Publishing, Inc.

Go on

No copying permitted.

Directions

Here is the article "Trapped in a Firestorm" that appeared in Test B. Read the article again, and then compare *your* answers with the answers given here. Read the *Strategies and Tips* to learn how to find the correct answers, and use the *Try It!* activities for additional practice.

Trapped in a Firestorm

On Storm King Mountain near Glenwood Springs, Colorado, fourteen white crosses stand among blackened trees. The crosses mark where firefighters fell during the worst United States wildfire disaster in modern history. With binoculars, Chuck Johnson can see the crosses from his back porch. "I think about the fire every time I look up there. And every time, I feel a sense of sadness."

A view of Storm King Mountain after the fire.

In the summer of 1994, after an unusually hot and dry spring, weather forecasters predicted a high risk for fire. Their predictions came true. By late June, wildfires were burning across Colorado and the West, and resources to fight them were running low. Storm King was covered with tall oak trees, pinion-juniper trees, and dead brush. When a severe lightning storm struck the mountain on July 2, a fire ignited. For two days, fire officials debated who should battle the blaze, yet no one hiked to the fire to assess the danger.

Residents nearby grew angry as they watched the fire spread. They feared the blaze would reach their homes, and they questioned why Storm King was not a high priority. On July 5, the Bureau of Land Management (BLM) sent a small crew up the mountain. It was a difficult climb, as the crew slipped on loose rocks, ran into near-vertical drop-offs, and got tangled in a maze of tree branches. By afternoon the firefighters had cleared a helicopter-landing site and started a fire line encircling the burning area. But after both of their chain saws broke, they called it quits and headed down the mountain. Meanwhile, an air tanker flew over the fire, dropping

©2002 Options Publishing, Inc.

No copying permitted.

INSTRUCTION

smoke jumpers:
forest firefighters who
parachute into locations
that are difficult to reach

retardant. The pilot made two passes, and then decided that a helicopter with a water bucket could do a better job. He turned back for home.

That night eight **smoke jumpers** parachuted onto Storm King. They hiked to the helicopter-landing site and saw that flames had spread across the fire line. With their headlamps on, they worked in the opposite direction, down the eastern slope. The terrain was steeper and rockier than they expected. In darkness it became too dangerous to stay on the rough slope, so they went back to the helicopter site and camped. A cool breeze blew over the mountaintop, and the crew sensed the weather was changing.

The next morning a cold front moved quickly toward Storm King. Forecasters issued a red flag warning for high, gusty winds, a serious alert for firefighters. But the smoke jumpers atop the mountain never received this warning. They had watched the fire grow overnight and knew they needed more help to bring it under control. They radioed for helicopters and two more crews, Hotshots if possible. Hotshots, a specially trained team, go where needed to fight fires.

Don Mackey, the smoke jumper in charge, learned that only one helicopter and one crew of Hotshots was available. Eight more smoke jumpers would also join the fight, along with a bigger BLM crew. The fire covered more than 125 acres. The team split into groups. Mackey led one group downhill—confident his plan for the fire could work, if the wind held off. The crew worked blindly in the summer heat. Dense vegetation and a small ridge blocked their view below. Even worse, their lookouts on the ridge could not see Mackey's team. The lookouts worried about the fighters' safety. In late afternoon, from atop the ridge, a column of smoke was spotted. The helicopter flew toward the area to drop water, but then the winds suddenly picked up. The new fire was rapidly spreading, and no amount of water could stop it. In a matter of minutes, swirling winds created an enormous firestorm that raced toward the firefighters on the slope. It moved faster than any human could run. Those who were closest to the ridge top survived. The other fourteen men and women, including Mackey, died where the flames overtook them.

An investigation of the incident blamed poor communication, a disregard for safety rules, and the "can-do" attitude of the firefighters for the Storm King tragedy.

A smoke jumper practices a landing.

©2002 Options Publishing, Inc.

Question 9   This question is about **identifying the main idea** of a selection. The *main idea* is the topic of a selection. It is the most important idea or thought that the author wants the reader to understand.

Strategies and Tips for Identifying the Main Idea

A **main idea** statement answers two questions:

- It tells you *who* or *what* the subject, or topic, of the selection is about. In "Trapped in a Firestorm," the main idea answers the question: *What is the subject, or topic?* The subject in this article is about a terrible fire on Storm King Mountain.
- It answers the question *does what?* or *is what?* or *how?* about the topic. In this article, the main idea statement answers *how* errors in judgment caused the deaths of fourteen firefighters.
- When you make a main idea statement, be sure that it is not *too broad* or *too narrow*. If you said this article was about forest fires, your statement would be *too broad*. It is too general and does not tell enough about the topic. If you said that the article was about smoke jumpers, the statement would be *too narrow*. This is a detail in the article.

9   **This article is mostly about**

Ⓐ   the dangers of fighting wildfires.   **Incorrect.** This statement is *too broad*. It is vague and does not tell much about the topic of the article.

Ⓑ   14 firefighters fought the fire on the mountain.   **Incorrect.** This statement is *too narrow*. It is a detail from the article.

Ⓒ   how Hotshots and smoke jumpers fight fires.   **Incorrect.** This statement is *too narrow*. It is one detail from the article.

Ⓓ   mistakes in judgment caused 14 deaths during a wildfire on Storm King Mountain.   **Correct. This describes the *main idea*. It tells you *what* the story is about and *how* the deaths occurred.**

TRY IT!   Below are four other titles for this article. Circle the title that best expresses the main idea. Then briefly explain why you chose that title.

A.   Don Mackey—Smoke Jumper   **B.**   Bureau of Land Management

C.   Colorado Fires   **D.**   Tragedy on Storm King Mountain

_____

_____

_____

INSTRUCTION

Go on

Question 10 This question is about **identifying supporting details**. *Supporting details* support, or build on, the main idea. They further explain, clarify, or examine the main idea.

Strategies and Tips for Identifying Supporting Details

Supporting details support, or build on, the main idea. To identify supporting details:

• Think about the main idea, or main point, the author gives you in the article. Read the last paragraph of "Trapped in a Firestorm." The author draws a conclusion about why the firefighters died. The details within the article help explain why the tragedy happened.

• Without supporting details, a main idea can be difficult to accept or understand. If you said that smoking was a foolish thing for anybody to do, you may not have made a convincing argument. Use facts or evidence to support your main idea. When you add **supporting details**—smoking can cause cancer and emphysema; research proves that second-hand smoke is dangerous; research proves that smokers have more long-term illness—you present facts that support your main idea. You now have a more convincing argument.

10 **Which detail from the article *best* supports the author's main idea?**

Ⓕ The BLM thought the fire would burn itself out.

Incorrect. Be sure to skim the article for details. You will see that this detail is not stated in the article.

Ⓖ Fire crews had difficulty climbing the rocky mountain.

Incorrect. This detail does not best support the main idea.

Ⓗ The fire was not a priority, and officials could not agree on who should fight it.

Correct. This best supports the main idea—this begins to describe why a series of mistakes led to the deaths.

Ⓙ An air tanker flew over the fire and dropped retardant.

Incorrect. This is also a minor detail from the article. It does not support the idea that a series of errors led to the death of the firefighters.

TRY IT! Reread the last, or concluding, paragraph in the article. List three details from the paragraph that support the author's conclusion.

_____

_____

_____

_____

_____

©2002 Options Publishing, Inc.

No copying permitted.

Question 11   This question is about **identifying cause-and-effect** relationships. A *cause* is an action that brings about a result, or *effect*.

Strategies and Tips for Identifying Cause and Effect

Sometimes, one event causes another event to happen. Authors use cause and effect to help you understand *why* something happens.

- One way to recognize a cause-and-effect statement is to look for words that *signal* the relationship: *because, therefore, since, before, after, as a result.* For example: *Maria's bicycle chain broke* (cause); <u>*as a result*</u>, *she had to walk home from school* (effect).

- Sometimes, the order is reversed and the effect comes before the cause: *Maria had to walk home from school* (effect) <u>*because*</u> *her bicycle chain broke* (cause).

11 **The firefighters on the side of the mountain died because**

Ⓐ they were not the fastest runners.   **Incorrect.** Nothing in the article says they died because they were not fast runners.

Ⓑ they were too far down the slope and could not outrun the fire.   **Correct. The firefighters died (effect) because they could not outrun the fire (cause).**

Ⓒ tree branches blocked their escape route.   **Incorrect.** This is not a cause mentioned in the article.

Ⓓ strong winds made it difficult for them to run fast.   **Incorrect.** Again, this is not a cause mentioned in the article.

TRY IT! Reread the **Strategies and Tips** box above. Then draws lines to match the correct cause-and-effect relationship. Skim the article for details that help you connect the relationship.

Cause	Effect
1. As the fire continued to spread,	the firefighters had a difficult climb.
2. Because the mountain side was covered with loose rocks, near-vertical drops, and tangled tree branches,	forecasters issued a high-wind warning.
3. Because a cold front was approaching the area,	nearby residents became concerned about their homes.

INSTRUCTION

©2002 Options Publishing, Inc.

Go on

Question 12   This question is about **drawing conclusions.** *Drawing conclusions* means making judgments based only on the *facts* that are presented in the selection.

Strategies and Tips for Drawing Conclusions

- A conclusion is never a wild guess. A **conclusion** is a decision or opinion that you make based on the *facts* that you have read.
- Make sure that the facts in the selection support your conclusion. For example: *As Maria looked at the large "C" at the top of her paper, disappointment spread across her face* (facts). You can logically conclude from the *facts* that Maria is disappointed by the grade of "C" on her paper.

12   **Why did the lookouts worry about the firefighters' safety?**

Ⓕ If a fire started nearby, the firefighters might not see it and might become trapped.

Correct. This is a logical conclusion from the *facts* **given. The firefighters could not see what was happening below them.**

Ⓖ They knew one helicopter was not enough to help them.

Incorrect. At this point in the article, the helicopter is not mentioned.

Ⓗ Their chain saws kept breaking.

Incorrect. This information does not support *why* they worried about safety.

Ⓙ They lost radio contact with their lookouts.

Incorrect. This is never hinted at in the story.

TRY IT! List two facts from the article that support this conclusion: In the summer of 1994, the resources for fighting fires in Colorado and the West were running low.

1. _____

_____

_____

2. _____

_____

_____

©2002 Options Publishing, Inc.

Question 13   This question is about **making inferences**. *Inferences* are logical guesses based on the evidence and details in the selection.

Strategies and Tips for Making Inferences

- When you do not have enough *facts* to lead you to a conclusion, you make an **inference**—a logical guess—from the details and information you are given. Writers often expect readers to make inferences. Authors do not always tell you what every character is feeling or why something has happened. You must infer what the writer has not directly stated by carefully examining the clues and details in a selection. When you make an inference, use the details from the story along with your knowledge and common sense about life.

- Read this sentence: *Ms. Lee, holding a stack of photocopies, left the school's print room and went to the principal's office.* You can logically infer that Ms. Lee works at the school—but you must not assume too much. You *cannot* infer that Ms. Lee is a teacher. The details do not support that inference. She might work as an office assistant.

13 You can infer that if the fire crews had received the red flag warning,

Ⓐ their plan of attack would have been different.

Correct. You know that the red flag warning means high winds. It is also clear in the article that the firefighters would have made other plans if they had known this very important detail.

Ⓑ more water drops would have been ordered.

Incorrect. The article directly states that once the wind picked up, no amount of water could stop the fire.

Ⓒ they would have called for weather updates.

Incorrect. They would know that the red flag warning means high winds. That details helps you infer that they would have changed their plans rather than call for weather updates.

Ⓓ they would have worked in larger groups.

Incorrect. The author does not give any details hinting that this would be a correct inference.

TRY IT! On the lines below, write the inference you can make about the helicopter from this statement: "The helicopter flew toward the area to drop water, but then the winds suddenly picked up. The new fire was spreading, and no amount of water could stop it."

_____

_____

_____

_____

INSTRUCTION

©2002 Options Publishing, Inc.

Question 14 This question is about **identifying details** from the selection. *Details* are the *who, what, when, where, why,* and *how* of what you have read. This type of question checks your basic understanding of the selection.

Strategies and Tips for Identifying Details

- **Details** in a selection help you organize the information that an author gives you. They also help you keep events in order. Details are different from supporting details. Supporting details help develop the main idea. **Details** are the basics—they tell you the **5Ws and H:** the *who, what, when, where, why,* and *how* of a story. Follow these steps to help you remember details:

- After you read the directions and introductory sentence to the selection, take a moment to **predict** what you might learn from the article. When you finish reading the selection, **reflect** on what you have read. **Reread** any parts of the selection that were unclear.

- Do not reread the entire story to look for details. Always skim the story to find the detail asked in the question.

14 **Where is Storm King Mountain located?**

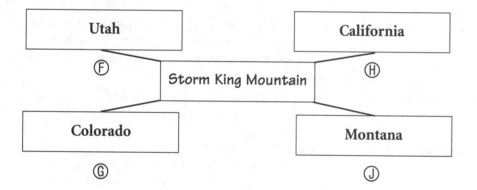

Answer G, *Colorado,* **is correct.**

Answers F, H, and J list incorrect locations. Skim paragraph 1 in the article to find the correct answer.

TRY IT! Write two details, or facts, that you learned from the article about firefighters.

1. _____

_____

_____

2. _____

_____

_____

©2002 Options Publishing, Inc.

No copying permitted.

Question 15   This question is about **identifying sequence**. Sequence is the particular order of a series of events or ideas.

Strategies and Tips for Identifying Sequence

- **Chronological order**, or time sequence, is the order in which events occur. Sometimes, the order of events is clear: One event simply follows the other. At other times, the author may use words that signal chronological order: *first, last, then, next, often.*
- Sequence is a kind of organization that helps you make sense of the events.
- Before you mark your final answer, be sure to read *all* the answer choices.

15 Who arrived *first* on the mountain to fight the fire?

Ⓐ the smoke jumpers   **Incorrect.** They were the second group to arrive.

Ⓑ residents who lived near the mountain   **Incorrect.** The residents never went up the mountain

Ⓒ the BLM crew   **Correct. This was the first crew sent up the mountain.**

Ⓓ the Hotshots   **Incorrect.** The Hotshots arrived *after* the BLM crew and the smoke jumpers.

TRY IT! "Trapped in a Firestorm" used chronological order and cause and effect to organize the facts. For example, because the spring had been unusually hot and dry (cause), the risk of forest fires was high (effect). The author uses a cause-and-effect pattern of organization.

On the lines below, give two more examples of cause-and-effect patterns that the author uses to organize the sequence of events in the article.

_____

_____

_____

_____

_____

_____

INSTRUCTION

Go on

©2002 Options Publishing, Inc.

No copying permitted.

Question 16 This question is about **identifying fact and opinion**. A *fact* can be proved. An *opinion* cannot be proved or disproved. An opinion is based on what someone thinks, feels, or believes.

Strategies and Tips for Identifying Fact and Opinion

- A **fact** is a statement that can be proved. It is supposed to be true or to have really happened. *Fourteen firefighters died on Storm King Mountain* is a fact. You can prove this statement by looking in a newspaper for the facts.
- An **opinion** is a statement about what someone feels or thinks. It cannot be proved or disproved. *The residents near Storm King were angry with the BLM* is an opinion. The word *angry* signals a feeling—and feelings are opinions. Words that describe how a person feels always signal an opinion: *sad, happy, angry, pleased, love, hate, beautiful,* or *wonderful.* An opinion tells what someone feels or believes.

16 **Which of the following statements is a fact?**

Ⓕ Hotshots are better trained than smoke jumpers.

Incorrect. This statement is an opinion: Who says that Hotshots are better trained than smoke jumpers?

Ⓖ Don Mackey loved his job.

Incorrect. This is a statement of how someone feels; therefore, it is an opinion.

Ⓗ The fire on Storm King was an awesome sight.

Incorrect. This is someone's opinion. Other people might not think it was an awesome sight.

Ⓙ Hot, dry weather conditions put Storm King at high risk for fire.

Correct. This statement can be proved by checking the facts.

TRY IT! On the lines below, rewrite each opinion statement above as a fact statement.
(Hint: Remember that what someone feels or believes signals an opinion.)

F. _____

G. _____

H. _____

©2002 Options Publishing, Inc.

No copying permitted.

Question 17 This question is about **identifying the genre** of a selection. The *genre* identifies the type of literary work, such as nonfiction, fiction, poetry, and drama. Each genre has its own unique characteristics.

 Strategies and Tips for Identifying Genre

Literary genre refers to the type of literature you read.

- **Fiction** is writing that uses characters and events that are not real. Myths, folktales, and many short stories are fiction.
- **Nonfiction** is writing that uses real people, places, and events. Articles, essays, biographies, autobiographies, and profiles are all nonfiction. They are about real people, places, or events.
- "Trapped in a Fire Storm" is an article. **Articles** inform or explain a subject to readers and are generally found in newspapers and magazines. Articles are usually objective; that is, they present facts rather than feelings or opinions.

17 "Trapped in a Firestorm" is a work of nonfiction because it

Ⓐ gives information about real people, places, or events.

Correct. Nonfiction gives information and facts about real people, places, or events.

Ⓑ develops fictional characters and events.

Incorrect. Fiction is writing about characters and events that are not real. This article presents real facts and events.

Ⓒ is passed down orally from one generation to the next.

Incorrect. This describes a folktale, which is a type of fiction.

Ⓓ teaches the reader a lesson about life.

Incorrect. This describes a fable, which is a type of fiction.

TRY IT! Review the **Strategies and Tips** box above. Then fill in the blanks below with the correct words.

1. Articles contain information about real _____, places, or events.

2. Articles are generally found in magazines and _____.

3. The facts and details in an article always support the _____.

Go on

©2002 Options Publishing, Inc.

INSTRUCTION

Question 18   This question is about understanding a word by **using context clues**. *Context clues* are found in the words and sentences before or after the unfamiliar word. They give clues, or hints, to the meaning of the unfamiliar word.

Strategies and Tips for Using Context Clues

Context clues refer to the words or sentences before or after an unfamiliar word.

- When you read, you are often faced with a word that you do not know. You can frequently determine what that word means by seeing how it is used in the sentence or in the paragraph. Sometimes, authors give you very specific clues.

- **Example clues:** The author gives you an example of the unfamiliar word. *Weather forecasters predicted a high risk for fire. Their predictions came true. By late June, wildfires were burning across Colorado and the West.* Notice that the author gives you an example to help you understand the meaning of *predicted* and *predictions* for a high risk of forest fires—"predictions came true . . . wildfires were burning across Colorado and the West."

- Before you mark the answer you think is correct, be sure to read *all* the choices.

---

18 "The *terrain* was steeper and rockier than they expected. In the darkness, it became too dangerous to stay on the rough slope." The word *terrain* means

Ⓕ fire.	**Incorrect.** This word does not make sense in the sentence. A fire is not "steeper" or "rockier."
Ⓖ river.	**Incorrect.** This is the opposite meaning of the word "terrain."
Ⓗ neighborhood.	**Incorrect.** You know that the firefighters were in the wilderness on the mountain. The word *neighborhood* does not make sense in the sentence.
Ⓙ land.	**Correct. The author gives examples of the terrain. It was "steeper and rockier" and "rough slope." These are examples of the land.**

TRY IT! Read these sentences below. Then circle the example clue in the sentence that helps define the underlined word.

1. Dense <u>vegetation</u> blocked their view. Trees and shrubs were so packed together that it was difficult for the firefighters to climb the mountain.

2. <u>Residents</u> who lived nearby grew angry as they watched the fire spread. People in the neighborhood met with the BLM.

Stop

No copying permitted.

©2002 Options Publishing, Inc.

Directions

Here is the story "The Lady or the Tiger?" that appeared in Test B.
Read the story again, and then compare *your* answers with the answers
given here. Read the *Strategies and Tips* to learn how to find the correct
answers, and use the *Try It!* activities for additional practice.

The Lady or the Tiger?

by Frank R. Stockton

Long ago, there lived a savage, cruel king, who believed that he was a
brilliant and reasonable sovereign. He also believed that justice was
best served in his arena, for he felt it improved the minds of his subjects.
In this arena, crime was punished and virtue was rewarded without the
aid of judges or juries. A person's guilt or innocence was decided by mere
chance. When a subject was accused of a crime, public notice was given
that on an appointed day the fate of the accused would be determined in
the king's arena.

On the appointed day, the king gave a signal and the accused stepped
out into the arena. Directly opposite him were two identical doors. It was
the duty of the subject to open one—he could open either door. From
one, a ferocious tiger might spring upon him as a punishment for his
guilt. From the other, a beautiful lady might step out and, as a reward of
his innocence, immediately marry the man. It was of no consequence that
he might already be wed. The king permitted no such arrangements to
interfere with his magnificent plan of punishment and reward.

This merciless king had a beautiful daughter—but she was as
arrogant and proud as her father was. Among the king's servants
was a handsome young man. It was not long before the princess fell
deeply in love with him. They met for many months until, one day,
the king learned of their love. He immediately threw the young
servant into prison and set a day for his trial.

The king chose a most savage tiger to crouch
behind one door and a beautiful servant girl to
stand behind the other. The young man would
die or marry—in either case, the king was rid of

©2002 Options Publishing, Inc.

INSTRUCTION

him. The trial day arrived, and the king gave the signal. The young man walked into the arena and bowed to the king, but the youth's eyes were fixed upon the princess.

From the moment of his arrest, the princess thought of nothing but this hour. For she had done what no other person had done—she had discovered the secret behind the doors. She knew behind which door the tiger paced and behind which the lady waited. The princess was familiar with the lady, who was one of the fairest and loveliest of the court—and the princess hated her. Often the princess had seen, or imagined that she had seen, the lady look with affection upon the young man, and the princess feared that the young man returned this look to the lady. Occasionally, the princess had seen them talking together—just for a moment or two—but the princess was jealous.

As the young man looked at the princess, he could tell she knew the secret. He had expected her to know, for she was his only hope. As their eyes met, the princess knew his question: "Which?" There was not an instant to be lost. The question was asked in a flash; it must be answered in another. She raised her hand, and made a slight, quick movement toward the right. No one but the young man saw it, and he walked rapidly across the empty space. He went directly to the door on the right and opened it.

Now, the point of the story is this: Did the tiger come out of that door, or did the lady?

The answer involves a study of the human heart. She had lost him, but who should have him? Often she cried out as she imagined her lover opening the door to meet the cruel fangs of the tiger! But how much oftener she imagined him opening the other door. Oh, how it pained her when she saw his look of delight as he met the lady! Her thoughts tortured her. She knew the young man would ask her, and she knew she would answer. And without the slightest hesitation, she had moved her hand to the right.

So, fair reader, which came out of the opened door—the lady or the tiger?

     No copying permitted.

©2002 Options Publishing, Inc.

Question 19   This question is about **identifying the main idea** of a selection. The *main idea* is the topic of a selection. It is the most important idea or thought that the author wants the reader to understand.

Strategies and Tips for Identifying the Main Idea

A **main idea** statement answers two questions:

* It tells you *who* or *what* the subject, or topic, of the selection is about. In "The Lady or the Tiger?," the main idea answers the question: *Who* is this story is about? It is about a princess and an important decision she must make.

* It answers the question *does what?* or *is what?* or *how?* about the topic. In this story, the main idea statement answers *does what*. The main idea explains *what* the princess must do, and what you must do. It presents *you* with a challenge. You must try to figure out which door the princess pointed to.

* When you make a main idea statement, be sure that it is not *too broad* or *too narrow*. If you said this story was about a princess, your statement is *too broad*. It is too general and does not tell enough about the topic. If you said that the article was about a trail, the statement is *too narrow*. This event is one small detail in the story.

19 **Which statement *best* describes the main idea of this story?**

Ⓐ The reader is challenged to guess the princess's decision.

Correct. This statement describes the *main idea*. It tells you *who* the story is about (the princess) and *what* you must do—you must figure out the answer.

Ⓑ Justice was not always fair in ancient times.

Incorrect. This statement is *too broad*. It is vague and does not tell much about the subject of the story.

Ⓒ Fierce tigers were used in the king's arena.

Incorrect. This is *too narrow*. It is a detail from the story.

Ⓓ The king was very cruel.

Incorrect. This is also *too narrow*. It is a detail from the story.

TRY IT! Make up another title for the story that expresses the main idea. Then explain the reasons you used to make up the title.

Go on

©2002 Options Publishing, Inc.

No copying permitted.

INSTRUCTION

Question 20   This question is about **identifying supporting details**. *Supporting details* support, or build on, the main idea. They further explain, clarify, or examine the main idea.

Strategies and Tips for Identifying the Supporting Details

Supporting details support, or build on, the main idea. To identify supporting details:

- Think about the **main idea**, or main point, the author is giving you in the story. In "The Lady or the Tiger?," the author presents you with a problem that *you* must figure out—which door did the princess point to? All the details within the story must support this main idea.
- Without **supporting details**, a main idea can be difficult to accept or understand. If you told your friends that you had a great time visiting relatives, you may not have convinced them. If you add supporting details—your cousins made great meals, they took you sightseeing and to a basketball game, the weather was great—your friends will *know* that you had a great time. These details support your main idea.

20 **Which detail from the story *best* supports the main idea?**

Ⓕ "A person's guilt or innocence was decided by mere chance."

Incorrect. This detail is important to the plot of the story, but it does not support the main idea—to figure out the princess's decision.

Ⓖ "This merciless king had a beautiful daughter . . ."

Incorrect. Again, this is a detail and does not best support the ending of the story.

Ⓗ "The king chose a most savage tiger to crouch behind one door . . ."

Incorrect. This is also a minor detail from the story.

Ⓙ "The answer involves a study of the human heart."

Correct. This best supports the main idea—that you are challenged to figure out which door the princess pointed to at the end of the story.

TRY IT! From what you know about the princess, which door do you think she pointed to: the lady or the tiger? Then list two details that support your decision.

_____

_____

_____

_____

_____

©2002 Options Publishing, Inc.

Question 21   This question is about **identifying sequence**. Sequence is the particular order of a series of events or ideas.

Strategies and Tips for Identifying Sequence

- **Chronological order**, or time sequence, is the order in which events occur. Sometimes, the order of events is clear: One event simply follows the other. At other times, the author may use words that signal chronological order: *first, last, then, next, often.*
- Sequence is a kind of organization that helps you make sense of the events.
- Before you mark your final answer, be sure to read *all* the answer choices.

21 **Which event happens *first* in the plot of the story?**

Ⓐ The king throws the young man into prison.

Incorrect. This happens *after* the king sees that the princess loves the young man.

Ⓑ The young man opens the door.

Incorrect. This event happens *last*.

Ⓒ The king discovers that the princess loves the young man.

Correct. This discovery begins the chain of events that places the young man in the arena.

Ⓓ The princess discovers the secret behind the doors.

Incorrect. This event happens *after* the young man is thrown into prison.

TRY IT! "The Lady or the Tiger?" uses chronological order and cause and effect to organize the events. For example, because the accused chose the door that had a tiger behind it, the accused died. The author uses a cause-and-effect pattern of organization.

Complete each of the sentences below using a cause-and-effect pattern to organize the sequence of events. Be sure to skim the story for the correct details.

1. Because the king discovered that the princess loved the young man, the young man

_____

2. Because the princess saw the young man and the lady talking together,

_____

Go on

©2002 Options Publishing, Inc.

INSTRUCTION

Question 22   This question is about **cause-and-effect** relationships. A *cause* is an action that brings about a result, or *effect*.

Strategies and Tips for Identifying Cause and Effect

Sometimes, one event causes another to happen. Authors use cause and effect to help you understand *why* something happens.

- One way to recognize a cause-and-effect statement is to look for words that signal the relationship: *because, therefore, since, before, after, as a result.* For example: *Gold was discovered in California* (cause); *as a result, thousands of people moved to California hoping to get rich* (effect).

- Sometimes, the order is reversed and the effect comes before the cause: *Thousands moved to California* (effect) *because gold was discovered there* (cause).

22   **The princess could save the young man's life because**

   Ⓕ   the princess could beg her father to save the young man.

     Incorrect. Nothing in the story hints that the princess could influence her father.

   Ⓖ   he knew that she loved him.

     Incorrect. This is not a true cause-and-effect statement. It does not tell *why* the young man looked to her for his life.

   Ⓗ   she knew behind which door the tiger sat.

     Correct. The man looked to her to save his life (effect) because the princess could show him which door meant death (cause).

   Ⓙ   the princess knew he loved the lady behind the door.

     Incorrect. If this were true, it probably would not save his life!

TRY IT! Reread the **Strategies and Tips** above. Then underline the **cause** and circle the **effect** in each of the following sentences. The first one is done for you.

1. (The temperature dropped rapidly) because a cold front moved through the area.

2. State funding for the library was cut; as a result, the library committee will raise money

   by holding a book sale.

3. Since Harry did not study for the test, his grade was very disappointing.

©2002 Options Publishing, Inc.

No copying permitted.

Question 23

This question is about **identifying generalizations**. A *generalization* is a broad statement intended to be true about a group of people, situations, or objects.

Strategies and Tips for Identifying Generalizations

Generalizations *should be* based on facts, but some generalizations are faulty and not based on facts.

- Generalizations are often signaled by clue words: *always, never, all, most,* or *many.* When you read a generalization, evaluate it to see if it is supported by facts, and rely on your own knowledge and experiences.

- A **valid generalization** is *Many flowers bloom in the spring,* or *all birds have wings.* Many flowers do bloom in spring, and birds do have wings. If the generalization is supported by facts, it is true, or valid.

- Writers sometimes make errors in reasoning when they try to prove a point. A **faulty generalization** is *All flowers bloom in spring.* If even one species of flower blooms at a different time, the generalization is faulty. A faulty generalization is untrue because it does not apply to *all* cases.

23 **Which of the following statements is a *valid* generalization?**

Ⓐ All the people enjoyed attending the event in the king's arena.

Incorrect. If even one person did not enjoy the event, the generalization is faulty.

Ⓑ Princesses are proud and cruel.

Incorrect. If even one princess in the world is humble and kind, this generalization is faulty.

Ⓒ The king always based his idea of justice on chance.

Correct. The story directly states that the king determined a person's guilt or innocence on which door he opened—pure chance. The king did not hear facts or weigh evidence. The accused had a fifty percent chance of opening the correct door.

Ⓓ Most of the accused people in the king's arena were guilty.

Incorrect. This is not valid. Since no evidence was heard, there is no way of knowing if a person was innocent or guilty.

TRY IT! Identify each generalization by writing either *faulty* or *valid* after the statement. Then explain why each is faulty or valid.

1. Politicians are always corrupt. _____

_____

2. Juries should weigh all the evidence before they present a verdict. _____

_____

©2002 Options Publishing, Inc.

Go on

INSTRUCTION

Question 24   This question is about **identifying the author's purpose** for writing. The *author's purpose* is the reason he or she wrote the selection.

Strategies and Tips for Identifying the Author's Purpose

An author usually has two purposes for writing—a **general purpose** and a **specific purpose**.

- The **general purpose** might be to entertain, to persuade, to inform, to explain, or to describe. "The Lady or the Tiger?" not only entertains you but also *describes* a puzzling problem that you must solve.
- The **specific purpose** is tied to the theme of the story and is the main point the author wants to make about the topic. Often, the author reinforces the specific purpose in the closing paragraph of the selection. The theme in this story is expressed in paragraph 8: "The answer involves a study of the human heart." The author asks you to use the details in the story and your knowledge of people to try to guess which door the princess indicated.

24 **What is the author's purpose in writing this story?**

Ⓕ to describe a question that makes readers think about human nature

> **Correct. This is the *author's main purpose.* The story builds to the point where he asks the question: Which came out of the opened door? You must use what you know about human nature to try to figure out the answer.**

Ⓖ to entertain readers with a humorous and amusing story

> **Incorrect.** This is not the author's main purpose. He wants you to think as well as to be entertained.

Ⓗ to persuade readers that life in ancient times was often cruel and unfair

> **Incorrect.** Through the details, the author does explain that, in this story's setting, the times were unfair. But his main purpose is to have you look at human nature.

Ⓙ to explain how the king administered justice

> **Incorrect.** This helps develop the plot, but it is not what the author wants you to learn. His focus is on the question itself.

TRY IT! To help identify the author's purpose for writing "The Lady and the Tiger?," answer the following questions.

1. What specific idea does the author want to communicate?

_____

2. How does the author want me to respond after reading the story?

_____

3. Do you think that the author accomplished his purpose? Explain.

_____

No copying permitted.

©2002 Options Publishing, Inc.

Question 25   This question is about understanding a word by **using context clues**. *Context clues* are found in the words and sentences before or after the unfamiliar word. They give clues, or hints, to the meaning of the unfamiliar word.

Strategies and Tips for Using Context Clues

Context clues refer to the words or sentences before or after the unfamiliar word. When you read, authors often use words that are unfamiliar to you. You can frequently determine what that word means by seeing how it is used in the sentence or in the paragraph. Sometimes, authors give you very specific clues:

- **Synonym clues:** A **synonym** is a word that means the same or nearly the same as the unfamiliar word. *The woman was horrified and* <u>*appalled*</u> *by the events in the king's arena.* The author helps you understand the word *appalled* by adding the synonym *horrified*.

- Before you mark the answer you think is correct, be sure to read *all* the answer choices.

25 "[The princess] was as *arrogant* and proud as her father was.
     The word *arrogant* means

Ⓐ violent.   **Incorrect.** This *might* seem correct at first, but read *all* the choices. You'll see that A is a much better answer.

Ⓑ conceited.   **Correct. The author gives you a clue to the meaning or *arrogant* by including the synonym *proud*. If you are *arrogant*, you are proud and conceited.**

Ⓒ humble.   **Incorrect.** The words *humble* and *proud* do not make sense together. They are opposites.

Ⓓ modest.   **Incorrect.** Again, *modest* and *proud* do not make sense used together in the sentence.

TRY IT! Working with a small group of classmates, make up your own multiple-choice questions for "The Lady or the Tiger?" Write a question for each of these skills: *Using Context Clues, Identifying Genre, Drawing Conclusions, Making Inferences,* and *Identifying Fact and Opinion.* Be sure that you can explain why each answer choice is correct or incorrect. Then exchange your test with another group and see if you can answer one another's questions.

Using Context Clues

_____

_____

_____

_____

_____

©2002 Options Publishing, Inc.

INSTRUCTION

Go on

Identifying Genre

_____

_____

_____

_____

Drawing Conclusions

_____

_____

_____

_____

Making Inferences

_____

_____

_____

_____

Identifying Fact and Opinion

_____

_____

_____

_____

Stop

No copying permitted.

©2002 Options Publishing, Inc.

Directions

In this part of the test, you will either read or listen to an article called "Christmas Eve Escape" and a letter written by Frederick Douglass called "Letter to Harriet Tubman." Then you will answer questions to demonstrate how well you understood what you read or how well you listened to what was read to you.

- If this is a Reading Session, your teacher will give you copies of the two selections.
- If this is a Listening Session, your teacher will read the selections to you. You will listen to the selections twice. The first time you hear the selections, listen carefully but do not take notes. When you listen to the selections the second time, you will take notes. Use your notes to answer the questions that follow. Use the space below and on the next page for your notes.

Here are the words and definitions you will need to know as you read or listen to "Letter to Harriet Tubman":

- **marked:** noticeably
- **wrought:** worked
- **multitude:** crowd of people

If this is a Listening Session, your teacher will now give you copies of the two letters. By studying the letters, the *Strategies and Tips*, and the sample answers, you will learn how to become a better listener and reader.

Strategies and Tips for Listening

- Determine your purpose for listening. Listen carefully as your teacher reads the brief introduction to each selection. Are you listening to remember facts and detailed information, or are you listening to make inferences and draw conclusions from a story that has characters, setting, and action? **Setting a purpose** for listening will help you get the most from the story you hear.
- Listen for **main ideas** and **details** that support those ideas.
- Let your **imagination** help you. As you hear the story, try to visualize the setting, characters, and action. You will remember more information if you let your mind create images.
- Finally, **listen carefully** as your teacher reads. Ignore any distractions around you.

Go on

©2002 Options Publishing, Inc.

No copying permitted.

Strategies and Tips for Note Taking

- The second time you listen to the selections read aloud, you will take notes. Taking notes helps you remember information, organize it, and use it to help you answer the questions that follow the stories.
- Use the **5Ws** and **H** to help you take notes. Think of the *who, what, when, where, why* and *how* as questions. Your notes are the **answers** to these questions.
- Use your **own words** to write your notes. Keep your notes as **brief** as possible. Use **short phrases** instead of complete sentences. Often, it is helpful to use a graphic organizer, such as a web or cluster map, a chart, or an outline.
- Use **symbols** or **abbreviations** when you can. For example, use *w/* for *with*; *&* for *and*; = for *equals*.

Notes

Sample Notes

Both leaders in the antisalvery movement

complete and accurate notes

Christmas Eve Escape	Letter to Harriet Tubman
Who is the story about? Harriet Tubman: Moses of her people	**Who?** Frederick Douglass—writer/speaker against slavery
What event happened? famous conductor of Underground RR—helped slaves escape	**What** event happened? compares his antislavery work with Tubman's
When did event happen? mid-1800s	**When** did event happen? mid-1800s
Where did event happen? Maryland	**Where** did event happen? don't know
Why did something happen? knew life as a slave—slavery evil—believed everyone deserved freedom. Knew importance of freedom to slaves	**Why** did something happen? he receives public praise for his work. Harriet receives only thanks of those she helps
How story ended or how **problem** was solved: led over 200 slaves to freedom—made people aware of evils of slavery	**How story** ended or how **problem** was solved: he wants to publicly praise her work/heroism

➡ **REMINDER** By turning the **5Ws** and **H** into questions, you have listed all the main ideas and the details that support those ideas.

©2002 Options Publishing, Inc.

Stop

No copying permitted.

26 Using specific details from the article, complete the chart below to compare Harriet Tubman with Moses.

Strategies and Tips for Identifying Supporting Details

- Imagine that you want to be a counselor this summer at a camp for young children. If you say to the owner of the camp, "I want to be a counselor," she might say, "OK. We'll get back to you." Without adding some **details** to **support** your main idea, you might not get very far. But what if you said, "I want to be a counselor because I like working with children. I really enjoy babysitting. I love to camp, hike, and swim. In fact, I have a lifesaving certificate in swimming from the local Y." These supporting details give solid reasons as to *why* you would like to work at the camp—and they might help convince the owner that you would be a good counselor. Main ideas are not very meaningful *unless* they are supported by details.

- In "Christmas Eve Escape," one main idea you are asked to explain is why Harriet Tubman was called the Moses of her people. Notice the details in the last paragraph of the story support that idea.

Harriet Tubman	Moses
antislavery leader	antislavery leader
led American slaves to freedom	led Hebrew slaves to freedom
strongly believed in freedom	strongly believed in freedom
led slaves from So. to No. and Canada	led slaves from Egypt to Canaan

complete and accurate chart

➡ **REMINDER** By comparing the specific details of Harriet's commitment to freedom with Moses' commitment to freedom, it is easy to understand why she is called the Moses of her people. The details support that idea.

TRY IT! One technique for remembering specific details is to form a picture, or visualize, the setting, characters, and action. On the lines below, describe the images that formed in your mind as you listened to "Christmas Eve Escape."

_____

_____

_____

_____

INSTRUCTION

Go on

©2002 Options Publishing, Inc.

No copying permitted.

27 Why do you think it was so important to Harriet Tubman to devote her life to running the Underground Railroad? Use information from the article to support your answer.

Strategies and Tips for Linking Main Ideas and Supporting Details

- The first step in answering Number 27 is to look back at your notes.
- Notice that under the heading "why," it is listed that Harriet knew what life was like as a slave. She also knew how important freedom was to slaves. These details *support* that main idea—that Harriet was committed to her work on the Underground Railroad.

Sample Response

good text details for support

Harriet Tubman personally knew what life was like as a slave. Her personal experiences helped her understand how important freedom was to slaves. She believed that every person deserved freedom. As a result, she committed her life to the Underground Railroad and leading slaves to freedom.

good transition

TRY IT! On the lines below, explain which detail in the article supports the idea that it was dangerous for Harriet Tubman to help runaway slaves.

_____

_____

_____

©2002 Options Publishing, Inc.

No copying permitted.

28 What does Douglass try to explain in his letter to Harriet Tubman? Use details from the letter to support your answer.

Strategies and Tips for Identifying Supporting Details

- **Supporting details** give you specific information that supports the main idea of the selection.
- The first step in using supporting details in your answer is to determine the main idea of the letter. In Number 28, you are asked to explain the main idea: "What the author tries to explain in his letter." The letter explains *that even though Douglass gets more praise and public attention, Harriet's work is just as important to the antislavery movement. She is an unsung hero of the cause.*
- Now you need to look for details in the letter that support that main idea. Ask yourself, "What details led me to conclude that the letter praises Harriet Tubman and her work?" Make a list of details:
  - Douglass works for movement in public and receives praise and encouragement.
  - Harriet works in private. Does not receive public encouragement.

Sample Response

good text details for support

Frederick Douglass's letter explains that he gets encouragement and praise from the public for his work in the antislavery movement, and he gets satisfaction from the public's approval. Harriet Tubman gets only a "God bless you" from the people she leads to freedom. His work is witnessed by the public. Her work is witnessed by "the midnight sky and the silent stars."

good use of relevant text support

➡️ **REMINDER** The supporting details listed in the box above are used in the answer.

TRY IT! Imagine that you are a slave who has just escaped to the north with the help of Harriet Tubman. On the lines below, write a brief letter to Harriet using details about the long journey to freedom.

_____

_____

_____

_____

©2002 Options Publishing, Inc.

No copying permitted.

Go on

INSTRUCTION

Planning Page

PLAN your writing for Number 29 here, but do NOT write your final answer on this page.
This page is for your use only. Your writing on this Planning Page will NOT count toward your
final score. Write your final answer beginning on the next page.

Answer

Strategies and Tips for Comparing and Contrasting

- **Comparing** means looking at the similarities between two or more things. **Contrasting** means looking at the differences between two or more things.

- In Number 29, you will compare and contrast the lives of Frederick Douglass and Harriet Tubman. You will look for similarities and differences between them. Comparing and contrasting characters can help you understand them better. Ask yourself: Did they do the same kind of work? How was their work the same? How was it different? Were their beliefs about their work the same?

Here is an example of an outline used to organize facts for Number 29.

I. *Comparison of the work that Tubman and Douglass did* (**main idea**)

  A. *Both worked for antislavery movement* (**important subtopic**)

    1. *Both former slaves* (**supporting detail**)

  B. *Douglass writer and speaker against slavery/Tubman famous conductor of*
   Underground RR (**important subtopic**)

    1. *Underground RR—secret escape route* (**supporting detail**)

II. *Contrast work of Douglass and Tubman* (**main idea**)

  A. *Douglass wrote and gave speeches* (**important subtopic**)

    1. *His work public* (**supporting detail**)

    2. *Got encouragement & praise from public* (**supporting detail**)

  B. *Tubman worked in secret* (**important subtopic**)

    1. *Public did not witness her work* (**supporting detail**)

    2. *Only reward heartfelt "God bless you"* (**supporting detail**)

III. *Infer Douglass's feelings toward Tubman* (**main idea**)

  A. *Admires her devotion to freedom* (**first important subtopic**)

    1. *Commitment to antislavery* (**supporting detail**)

  B. *Respects her heroism* (**second important subtopic**)

    1. *Takes risks to help people escape slavery* (**supporting detail**)

➥ **REMINDER** In Number 29, you are asked to include these main ideas: *comparison of the work that each person did, contrast the work that they did, and infer Douglass's feelings toward Tubman.* Note that the Roman numerals match the main ideas you must include in your essay.

©2002 Options Publishing, Inc.

No copying permitted.

29 From what you have learned in these two selections, compare and contrast the lives of

Frederick Douglass and Harriet Tubman.

In your discussion, be sure to include

- a comparison of the work that each person did
- a contrast of their work
- what you can infer about Douglass's feelings toward Harriet Tubman

Check your writing for correct spelling, grammar, paragraphs, and punctuation.

Strategies and Tips for Writing

- Now it is time to turn your outline into an essay.
- The first step is to look at your outline and the three main ideas listed for Roman numerals I., II., and III. Each main idea becomes a paragraph. Each main idea also becomes the **topic sentence**—a sentence that states the main idea of a paragraph—for each paragraph. Notice that in the answer below, each topic sentence is in boldfaced type.
- Notice also that all the other sentences in the paragraphs are **details** that support the topic sentences.

Sample Response   *topic sentence*

   Both Frederick Douglass and Harriet Tubman, who were former slaves, were a part of the antislavery movement. The antislavery movement made people aware of the evils of slavery, and it also tried to end the practice of slavery. Frederick Douglass was a writer and speaker for the movement. Harriet Tubman was one of the most famous conductors of the Underground Railroad, which was a secret escape route for slaves.

   Although Frederick Douglass and Harriet Tubman both worked to end slavery, they had different roles in the antislavery movement. Frederick Douglass wrote for and spoke to the public. His work was done for the public, and he received encouragement and praise, which gave him satisfaction. Harriet Tubman, on the other hand, worked in secret. The public did not witness her work to end slavery. She directly helped slaves gain freedom by leading them to free states in the North and to Canada.

topic sentence

good supporting details for topic sentences

Go on

©2002 Options Publishing, Inc.

INSTRUCTION

topic sentence

We can infer from Frederick Douglass's letter that he respected and admired Harriet Tubman. He says that his reward is public praise. Her reward is a heartfelt "God bless you" from the people she guided to freedom. He admires her devotion to freedom and her heroism.

insightful response—goes beyond the text

TRY IT! Practice how well you remember the article "Christmas Eve Escape." Without looking back at the selection, briefly retell the story in your own words. When you finish, compare your version with the selection. How well did you remember the main ideas and supporting details?

Stop

©2002 Options Publishing, Inc.

No copying permitted.

Here is the article "The Fight for Equality" and the poem "See It Through" that appeared in Test B. Read the selections again, and then compare *your* answers with the answers given here. Read *Strategies and Tips* to learn how to find the correct answers, and use the *TRY IT!* activities for additional practice.

Now begin reading.

The Fight for Equality

It is Election Day in Rochester, New York. The polls are open and United States citizens stand in line to vote for the next president of the United States. Among those in line are sixteen women voting for the first time. They cast their ballots and leave the polling place. Three weeks later, all sixteen women are arrested.

The women, led by Susan B. Anthony, were all citizens of the United States, but the year was 1872. Women could not legally vote.

In 1868, the Fourteenth Amendment to the Constitution was passed. It stated that all people born in the United States were citizens and that no citizen could be denied legal privileges. Anthony and several other women thought it was time to put this law to a test by voting. They felt they deserved the same civil and political rights as American men. Anthony, the most famous and outspoken, was the only one in the group that was ordered to stand trial.

While awaiting her trial, Anthony traveled across the country speaking out against the way women were viewed and treated in American society. Finally, on June 17, 1873, Anthony did stand trial. But the judge, who opposed women's suffrage, made his decision before the trial even began. He did not allow Anthony to testify on her own behalf. He ordered the jury to find her guilty of violating voting laws. He also fined her $100—a fee she refused to pay and remains unpaid to this day. Anthony knew that if she were put in prison for not paying the fine, she would be able to test the law by having a new trial. The judge also knew this, and he did not imprison her for failing to pay the fine. This denied her the chance to appeal the court's decision and challenge the Fourteenth Amendment.

Susan B. Anthony

©2002 Options Publishing, Inc.

No copying permitted.

Anthony's brush with the law did not discourage her from continuing the campaign for equality. In fact, little in her life had ever discouraged this determined woman. Born to Quaker parents in 1820, Anthony experienced freedom and respect that many other girls were denied growing up in the United States. Quakers were among the first groups to practice full equality for the sexes and the races. Anthony's parents were strong supporters of the temperance (avoidance of alcohol) and the abolitionist (antislavery) movements. Quakers believed that slavery was morally wrong. They helped to organize and operate the Underground Railroad, which helped slaves escape to Canada. In her parents' home, Anthony learned independence, courage, and a passion for justice. Everyone in the Anthony home was dedicated to the movement to end slavery. It was the abolitionists and their actions who forced the nation to deal with the issue of slavery.

At seventeen, Anthony finished school and took her first paying job as a teacher, where her salary was about one-fifth of what male teachers made. Anthony thought this was unfair. When she protested and asked for equal pay, she lost her job. She found another teaching position. And she continued the fight to free all slaves immediately.

At an antislavery meeting in 1851, she met a woman who became a life-long friend and political partner—Elizabeth Cady Stanton. The two also supported temperance—laws that prohibit the sale of alcohol. They spoke out against the abuse of women and children by men who were alcoholics. At a temperance meeting, Anthony was not allowed to speak because she was a woman. She was told by the men to "listen and learn." In Anthony's upbringing, everyone in the family was allowed to express an opinion. It was after that meeting that she vowed to join Stanton and dedicate herself to gaining rights for women. Despite the horrible and unjust things said about her in the newspapers, Anthony continued to travel and make public speeches supporting women's rights.

©2002 Options Publishing, Inc.

No copying permitted.

In 1866, Anthony and Stanton founded the American Equal Rights Association. Three years later, a large portion of the group broke away to form their own group called the American Woman Suffrage Association. The main difference between the groups was their approach to achieving the vote. Stanton and Anthony wanted to gain the vote for women on the national level. The new group wanted to gain the vote on a state-by-state basis.

Anthony worked for women's rights up until the day she died—March 13, 1906. When she died, women could vote in only four states—Wyoming, Colorado, Idaho, and Utah.

On June 4, 1919, fourteen years after Anthony's death, the Nineteenth Amendment was passed, giving women the right to vote.

Amendment 19 to the Constitution

Section 1. The right of citizens of the United States to vote shall not be denied or abridged by the United States or by any state on account of sex.

INSTRUCTION

Go on

©2002 Options Publishing, Inc.

No copying permitted.

30 Complete the chart with words or phrases that describe Susan B. Anthony's character. Identify information from the article that supports each character trait.

Strategies and Tips for Understanding Character Traits

- **Character traits** are the qualities that make up a person's personality.
- You probably know people who are cheerful and upbeat, people who are somber or serious, or people who are generous or miserly. You decide what qualities, or character traits, people have by listening to their words and statements and observing their actions.
- In literature, you learn about a character's traits almost the same way. You read what he or she says, what he or she does, or what he or she thinks. A character's words, actions, and thoughts reinforce, or support, that character trait.

Sample Response

complete and accurate chart

Character Trait	Supporting Information
Independent or Self-confident	Ignores the unjust and horrible things said about her in the newspaper and continues her work for women's rights
Dedicated *good supporting information*	Thought that it was unfair for male teachers to get higher pay, and she protested. She is annoyed that she is not allowed to speak at the temperance meeting but does not give up. She vows to work for women's rights
Determined or Persistent	Never gave up the fight against slavery; fought for women's right to vote; made public speeches

TRY IT! Look at the supporting information for each of Susan B. Anthony's character traits in Number 30. Next to each character trait listed below, explain how you learned about that trait—through her *words*, *actions*, or *thoughts*.

1. Independent: _____

2. Dedicated: _____

3. Determined: _____

©2002 Options Publishing, Inc.

No copying permitted.

31 How did Anthony feel about slavery and the use of alcohol? Explain your answer using details from the article.

Strategies and Tips for Making Inferences About Character Traits

• An inference is a conclusion you make based on specific facts. You can often make an inference about a character's personality from details given in the selection. These details may come from the character's thoughts, words, or actions.

Sample Response

addresses all parts of question

Susan B. Anthony felt that [slavery was morally wrong and that all slaves should be freed immediately.] Anthony also believed that there [should be laws to stop or limit the sale of alcohol.] She believed that the use of alcohol increased the abuse against women and children.

➡ **REMINDER** By examining Anthony's feelings about slavery and alcohol, you can infer that one of her character traits is *dedication*. She fights against slavery, which she believes is morally wrong, and she fights for the rights of women and children by trying to limit the sale of alcohol.

TRY IT! What can you infer about Susan B. Anthony's personality from this quotation from the article: "Anthony knew that if she were put in prison for not paying the fine, she would be able to test the law by having a new trial"? Write your answer on the lines below.

_____

_____

_____

_____

_____

_____

INSTRUCTION

Go on

©2002 Options Publishing, Inc.

No copying permitted.

See It Through

Edgar A. Guest

When you're up against a trouble,
Meet it squarely, face to face;
Lift your chin and set your shoulders,
Plant your feet and take a brace.
When it's **vain** to try to dodge it,
Do the best that you can do;
You may fail, but you may conquer,
See it through!

> **vain:** unsuccessful; useless

Black may be the clouds about you
And your future may seem **grim**,
But don't let your nerve desert you;
Keep yourself in fighting trim.
If the worst is bound to happen,
Spite of all that you can do,
Running from it will not save you,
See it through!

> **grim:** cheerless

Even hope may seem but **futile**,
When with troubles you're **beset**,
But remember you are facing
Just what other men have met.
You may fail, but fall still fighting;
Don't give up, whate'er you do;
Eyes front, head high to the finish.
See it through!

> **futile:** useless

> **beset:** attacked on all sides

No copying permitted.

©2002 Options Publishing, Inc

32 What is most likely the poet's main purpose in writing this poem? Use ideas from the poem to support your answer.

Strategies and Tips for Identifying the Author's Purpose

- To identify an **author's purpose**, ask yourself: What is the author's general objective— how does the author want me to respond? What specific ideas does the author want me to understand?
- The **general purpose** might be to entertain, to persuade, to inform, to explain, or to express feelings or thoughts.
- The **specific purpose** is tied to the theme. The specific purpose is the main point the author wants to make about the topic.

Good! Shows you went back to poem to add support.

Sample Response

The poet's main purpose is to tell people not to give up on their goal when they face trouble or when things seem to be going wrong. He says, "You may fail, but you may conquer, See it through!" He is saying that if you don't try to make your goal, you will never know if you could have succeeded. When you believe in something, "See it through!"

TRY IT! To help determine the poet's purpose, answer these questions:

1. How does the poet want me to respond? _____

_____

2. What specific ideas does the poet want to convey to me? _____

_____

3. What is the poet's attitude, or feelings, toward the subject? _____

_____

INSTRUCTION

Go on

©2002 Options Publishing, Inc.

Planning Page

PLAN your writing for Number 33 here, but do NOT write your final answer on this page.
This page is for your use only. Your writing on this Planning Page will NOT count toward your final score. **Write your final answer beginning on the next page.**

Answer

Strategies and Tips for Applying Themes

- A **theme** is a central message or purpose of a selection. A theme is often expressed as a **general statement** about human nature or about life.
- The first step in planning your answer for Number 33 is to make sure that you understand the themes, or messages, in "The Fight for Equality" and "See It Through."
- To discover the theme of a story or a poem, think about the feelings you have *as* you read the selections and *after* you read them. Ask yourself these questions: Did the events or images remind me of things that have happened in my life of the life of someone I know? What do the two selections tell me about human nature or life?
- Finally, look for details in the selection that support the theme.

Sample Notes

Here is one way to organize your thoughts:

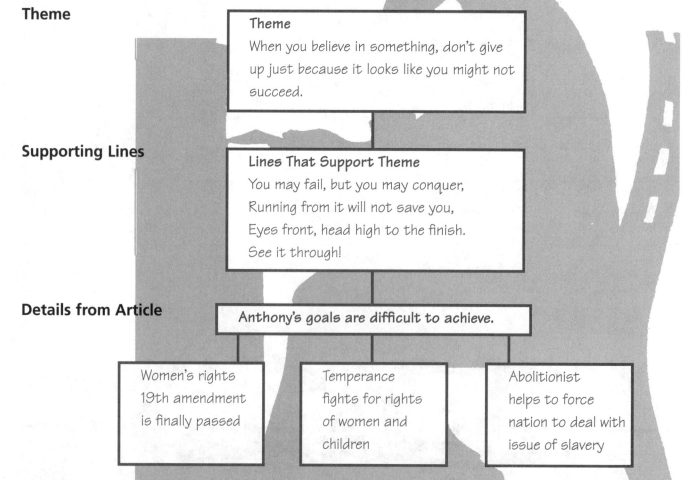

Theme

> **Theme**
> When you believe in something, don't give up just because it looks like you might not succeed.

Supporting Lines

> **Lines That Support Theme**
> You may fail, but you may conquer,
> Running from it will not save you,
> Eyes front, head high to the finish.
> See it through!

Details from Article

> Anthony's goals are difficult to achieve.

> Women's rights
> 19th amendment
> is finally passed

> Temperance
> fights for rights
> of women and
> children

> Abolitionist
> helps to force
> nation to deal with
> issue of slavery

©2002 Options Publishing, Inc.

No copying permitted.

33 Choose a line or lines from the poem. Discuss the meaning of your selection, and explain how it applies to Susan B. Anthony. Use ideas from BOTH the poem and the article in your answer. In your answer, be sure to include

- the line or lines you have selected from the poem
- an explanation of how your selection applies to Susan B. Anthony

 Check your writing for correct spelling, grammar, paragraphs, and punctuation.

support shows through understanding of text

Sample Response   *good choice of lines from poem*

The poem "See It Through," by Edgar A. Guest, relates to the champion of women's rights Susan B. Anthony. The lines that especially relate are these: "You may fail, but you may conquer, Running from it will not save you, Eyes front, head high to the finish. See it through!" These lines relate to Susan B. Anthony. She had a passion for justice and fought to make life better for slaves, women, and children. She set her goals and never gave up even when the newspapers said unfair things about her. Anthony's work in the abolitionist movement helped the nation face the issue of slavery. Her work in the temperance movement helped people understand that women and children were being abused, and her work for women's rights led to the Nineteenth Amendment that gave women the right to vote. Susan B. Anthony did "See it through!"

good conclusion/connection

Go on

©2002 Options Publishing, Inc.

INSTRUCTION

TRY IT! Reorganize the ideas you wrote about on page 61 for Number 33 by using the Main Idea/Supporting Details graphic organizer below.

Main Idea/Supporting Details

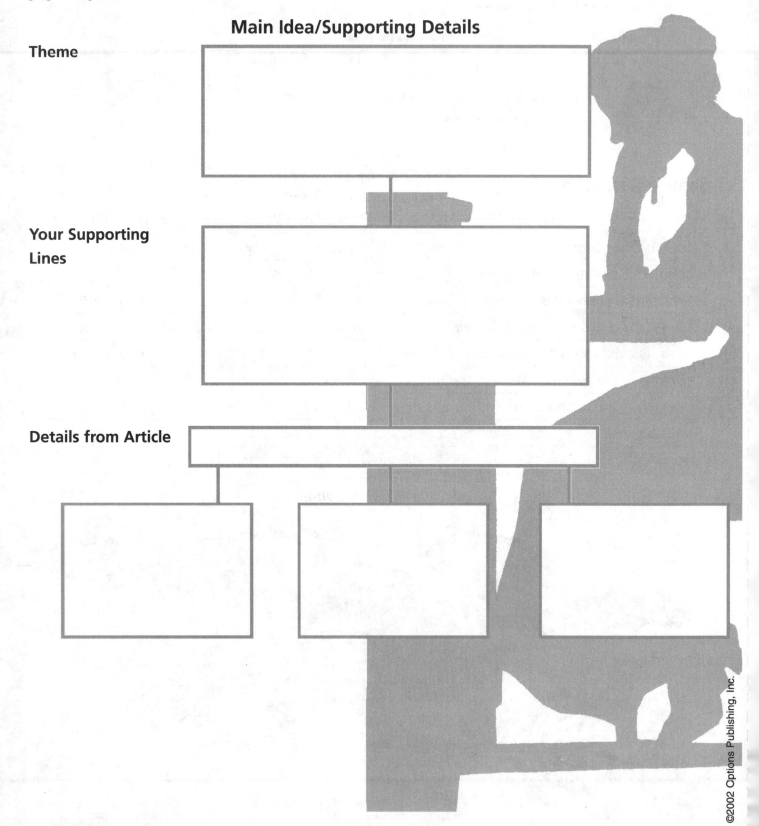

Theme

Your Supporting Lines

Details from Article

No copying permitted.

©2002 Options Publishing, Inc.

Planning Page

PLAN your writing for Number 34 here, but do NOT write your final answer on this page.
This page is for your use only. Your writing on this Planning Page will NOT count toward your final score. Write your final answer beginning on the next page.

☼ Strategies and Tips for Outlining/Writing

Outlining helps you formally organize your ideas, but a **basic outline pattern** also provides a helpful form in which to write down your ideas as you think of them.

- Start by writing down some main ideas you want to include in your essay. For your essay, the **main ideas** you will include are listed in Number 34. Under each main idea, jot down **supporting details**.
- Notice that the main ideas listed in Number 34 are written as questions on this Planning Page.

Sample Notes

I. **Introduction:** *Who* is the person and *what* did the person do?
- Rosa Parks
- In 1955, Parks refused to give up her seat on the city bus to a white passenger.
- "Our mistreatment was just not right, and I was tired of it."
- She broke the segregation laws.

II. **Body:** *What* difficulties did the person face?
- She was arrested and sent to jail
- African-Americans began boycott of city buses. Martin Luther King, Jr. led movement. Marking beginning of the civil rights movement.
- Parks lost job as seamstress because of boycott.

III. **Body:** *How* did person overcome the difficulties?
- By refusing to give up seat, broke law.
- Refused to pay fine to bring her case to court.
- In court, she would challenge the Montgomery segregation law.

IV. **Conclusion:** Summarize the results of the person's goal
- U.S. Supreme Court ruled that Montgomery law was illegal.
- Other cities followed Park's example.
- Parks "the mother of the civil rights movement."

Go on

©2002 Options Publishing, Inc.

TRY IT! On the lines below, rewrite the notes *you* made for *your* essay topic. Use the notes you wrote for the Planning Page on page 64. Use the basic outline pattern you read about on page 173.

_____

_____

_____

_____

_____

_____

_____

_____

_____

_____

_____

_____

_____

_____

_____

_____

_____

_____

_____

_____

_____

_____

_____

_____

©2002 Options Publishing, Inc.

No copying permitted.

34 Write an essay about a person in history or someone *you* know who has overcome obstacles to achieve an important goal.

In your essay, be sure to include

- who the person is
- what he or she did
- the difficulties he or she faced
- how the difficulties were overcome
- an introduction, a body, and a conclusion

Check your writing for correct spelling, grammar, paragraphs, and punctuation.

good use of quotation

Good use of supporting details. You've answered all aspects of the question.

Sample Response

"Our mistreatment was just not right, and I was tired of it." With those thoughts in her mind, Rosa Parks refused to give up her seat on a city bus to a white passenger. The place was Montgomery, Alabama, and the year was 1955. Parks was breaking the segregation laws in Montgomery. She was legally required to move if a white person wanted the seat.

The bus driver called the police and had her arrested. Parks was taken to the police station, fingerprinted, and jailed. She made her one call to an NAACP (National Association for the Advancement of Colored People) lawyer. When African Americans found out that Rosa Parks had been arrested and jailed, they decided to boycott the city buses until segregation was stopped. Martin Luther King, Jr., helped to organize the boycott. The boycott lasted for 382 days. With thousands of African Americans refusing to ride the buses, the bus company lost a great amount of money.

Not only did Parks lose her job because of the boycott, she was also charged a fine for breaking the law. But like Susan B. Anthony, Parks refused to pay it. She knew that if she were jailed, there would have to be a trial. Then the segregation laws would be challenged in court.

Go on

©2002 Options Publishing, Inc.

In 1956, the U. S. Supreme Court ruled that the Montgomery segregation laws were illegal. Other cities soon followed Rosa Park's example and protested the segregation laws. Rosa Parks' determination to "see it through" has earned her the title of "mother of the civil rights movement."

> *Conclusion goes beyond question—shows insight. Nicely ties in poem and article.*

TRY IT! In the TRY IT! on page 174, you reorganized the notes you make for the topic *you chose* to write about for Number 34. You probably have more information, or that information is better organized. Now that you have reorganized your notes with added information, rewrite your essay on the lines below. Be sure that you include an introduction, a body, and a conclusion in your essay.

When you are finished, exchange your essay with a classmate's. Using what you have learned about organizing ideas for writing, comment on each other's essays.

_____

_____

_____

_____

_____

_____

_____

_____

_____

_____

_____

_____

_____

Stop

©2002 Options Publishing, Inc.

No copying permitted.